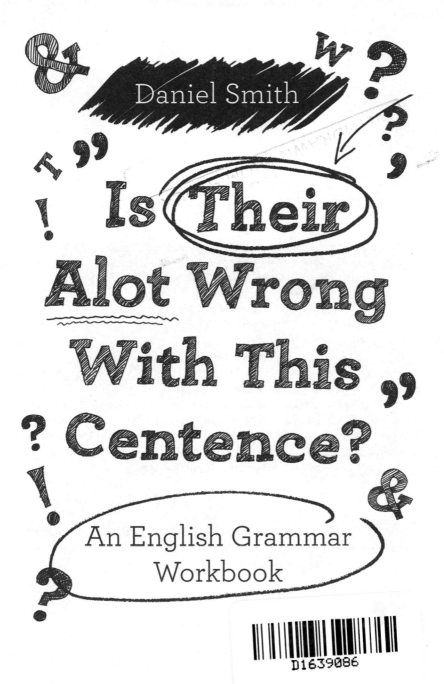

Daniel Smith

Is Their Alot Wrong With This Centence?

An English Grammar Workbook

Michael O'Mara Books Ltd

First published in Great Britain in 2011 by
Michael O'Mara Books Limited
9 Lion Yard
Tremadoc Road
London SW4 7NQ

A CIP catalogue record for this book is available from the British Library.

Papers used by Michael O'Mara Books Limited are natural, recyclable products
made from wood grown in sustainable forests. The manufacturing processes
conform to the environmental regulations of the country of origin.

ISBN: 978-1-84317-714-2

1 3 5 7 9 10 8 6 4 2

Designed and typeset by www.glensaville.com

Printed and bound CPI Group (UK), Croydon, CR0 4YY

www.mombooks.com

ACKNOWLEDGEMENTS

My thanks first to my editor, Toby Buchan, and Louise Dixon and the rest of the Michael O'Mara team who have whipped this book into shape. I have also made regular reference to several exceedingly helpful volumes. These include:

Concise Oxford English Dictionary, OUP, 2006

Lamb, Bernard, *The Queen's English: And How to Use It*, Michael O'Mara Books, 2010

Murphy, Raymond, *Essential Grammar in Use (Third Edition)*, Cambridge University Press, 2007

Scrivenor, Patrick, *I Used to Know That: English*, Michael O'Mara Books, 2010

Taggart, Caroline, & Wines, J. A., *My Grammar and I (or should that be 'Me'?)*, Michael O'Mara Books, 2008

Trask, R.L., *The Penguin Dictionary of English Grammar*, Penguin, 2000

Finally, as ever, thanks to Rosie.

For Rosie

CONTENTS

INTRODUCTION

There is the old joke about Little Jimmy, whose teacher asks him what he has done over the weekend.

'Me and my mum goed into town on the bus and done our shopping,' says Jimmy.

'Where's your grammar, Jimmy?' asks his appalled teacher.

'Oh, she's sat at home watching *Countdown*. It's alright though, cos Mum done her shopping too.'

As well as being a golden oldie, it does highlight the somewhat loose relationship that much of the world maintains with the formal rules of language. Even if we are able to recall from our schooldays something of what verbs and nouns are (or even adjectives and adverbs, at a push), only the truly blessed are likely to feel comfortable with countables and non-countables, misplaced modifiers and (horror of all horrors) the subjunctive.

The great beauty of English is its richness, which comes from myriad influences that have acted upon it over millennia. Alas, the counterpoint to that richness is complexity. The truth is that the English language is complicated, its grammar beset with exceptions and irregularities that can easily send the mind into an uncontrollable spin. However, try to think of grammar as representing rules to guide you rather than regulations designed to trip you up. (Notice how I've ended a sentence with a preposition! When you know the rules, feel free to break the odd one here and there if you think it improves your expression.)

Grammar, after all, is about accuracy and not pedantry. It is about honing your communication, not stifling it. The quizzes in this workbook are designed to give you a thorough workout across the range of grammatical components, from parts of speech to punctuation, sentence construction, style and more. I have generally assumed some level of knowledge of the language (this is not the book for absolute beginners), but where it seemed apposite, I have included a few background notes to arm you for the particular challenge ahead.

Crucially, I hope the quizzes are fun. Some are relatively simple, others truly taxing. Whether you're a foreign student or simply hoping to reawaken all that knowledge left behind in the classroom, some of the content you'll find here deals with highly nuanced grammatical points over which even the experts may still be slugging it out. It does not matter if you get some questions wrong – that is when you will learn most.

Let the grammatical games begin!

THE QUIZZES

Spare Parts:
Parts of Speech

To begin with the obvious, language is mostly made up of words. There are, of course, a few other bits and pieces, such as numbers and punctuation marks, thrown in for good measure, but it is words that are the main building blocks. When we are very young and picking up our first vocabulary we tend to think that a word is just a word. Then we go to school and discover that every word can be classified into one of many groups that we call 'parts of speech'. Then we leave school, forget all that and return once more to the 'a word is just a word' theory. So let's see how much you can dredge up from your memory about the parts of speech.

Quiz 1

Below are three lists. In Column A are listed the most basic parts of speech (which we shall look at in more detail over the coming pages). In Column B is a list of simple definitions explaining what each part of speech does; and in Column C some random examples from each group. To get you warmed up, simply match the definition to the correct part of speech and then find the examples of each.

Answers on page 177

21

1)	noun	a 'joining' word that links together sentences, phrases or clauses	I, him, something
2)	verb	a 'stand-alone' word that expresses emotion	at, in, near
3)	pronoun	a 'naming' word for a person, thing or place	to have, to run, to eat
4)	adjective	a word that describes a noun	boo, hurray, ouch
5)	adverb	a word used before a noun or pronoun to express the relationship between it and another object	green, funny, sad
6)	preposition	a word that adds meaning to a verb	and, but, until
7)	conjunction	a 'doing' word that describes an action or a state of being	eagerly, fast, freely
8)	interjection	a word used as a substitute for a noun, usually referring to a participant in the sentence or a noun already mentioned	house, man, New York

Quiz 2

OK, now here's a series of simple tests to see how good you are at identifying the various parts of speech. Each part is contained in five sentences. In the first test, mark all of the nouns that you can see. In the next, mark all the verbs, and so on.

a) Nouns

1) The day is long.
2) My dad loves a good book.
3) The dog went to the vet.
4) The man ran round the park.
5) Teachers work in schools.

b) Verbs

1) Dave runs each morning.
2) Sometimes I see Dave on my way to work.
3) My dog loves everyone he meets.
4) We have visited the Taj Mahal.
5) I will be finishing my studies next month.

c) Pronouns

1) I like chocolate cake.
2) Jessica simply ignored her.
3) I like this but I don't like those.
4) He trusted himself implicitly.
5) I don't think much of yours!

d) Adjectives

1) The sky was full of twinkling stars.
2) He made a clumsy attempt to kiss his date.
3) She was impressed by the helpful shop attendant.

Answers on page 178

4) We were put off our dinner by the boorish group of businessmen.

5) We basked in the glow of the golden sun.

e) Adverbs

1) The driver pointed at me angrily.

2) The choir sang angelically.

3) The man stumbled drunkenly into the doorway.

4) She applied her make-up gaudily.

5) She fell to the floor, sobbing melodramatically.

f) Prepositions

1) I stood near the bar.

2) The athlete ran round the track.

3) We sailed far beyond the island.

4) They left during the interval.

5) The wolf ran through the woods.

g) Conjunctions

1) He looked both ways and then crossed the road.

2) I'm not going out until the rain stops.

3) Either the dog goes or I do.

4) He went to the bank in order that he could withdraw his savings.

5) Sheila said she would go to the party as long as Kev wasn't there.

h) Interjections

1) Good grief! There are lots of things to do.

2) As she waved, she called out 'Goodbye!'

3) When asked if he would pass the exam, he replied 'Yes!'

4) 'Encore!' cried out the audience.

5) 'Shh!' the librarian demanded of the noisy visitor.

Quiz 3

Too easy? Well, have a look at the short passage below and then try to label every word correctly.

When (_____) I (_____) was (_____) a (_____) child, (_____) I (_____) loved (_____) to (_____) learn (_____) new (_____) words (_____) but (_____) only (_____) now (_____) am (_____) I (_____) starting (_____) to (_____) understand (_____) the (_____) complexities (_____) of (_____) the (_____) language. (_____) Wow, (_____) thank (_____) goodness (_____) that (_____) I (_____) have (_____) this (_____) book (_____) close (_____) by (_____) to (_____) help (_____) me (_____)!

The Noun's the Thing: Nouns

Nouns are the words we use to name things. Along with verbs, they are the parts of speech we really could not function without. As you'd expect, there are quite a few nouns that work in subtly different ways. The two basic types are:

- common nouns: used to name a person, animal, place, thing or abstract concept. These are subdivided into:

Answers on page 179

- concrete nouns – used to describe things that can be recognized by at least one of the senses (e.g. a car or a dog or a turnip or an alarm)
- abstract nouns – which describe something outside of the physical (e.g. fear or joy).
- proper nouns: used to name a specific person, animal, place or thing, and usually identifiable by the presence of a capital letter (e.g. the Houses of Parliament or Mount Everest or Lady Gaga).

Quiz 4

Let's see how good you are at spotting the different types of noun. In the sentences below, a noun is indicated in bold type. Mark whether you think it is a concrete, abstract or proper noun.

1) She is a **pleasure** to work with.
2) The **Queen** was on an official trip.
3) He was attacked by a **squid**.
4) I want to play football for **Everton**.
5) I have a pain in my **leg**.
6) We flew across the **Atlantic Ocean**.
7) The mourners were full of **grief**.
8) The shaman sacrificed a **goat**.
9) She had a fear of **failure**.
10) You are staying in **Kathmandu**.

Answers on page 179

Compounding the Problem: Compound Nouns

A compound noun is a noun made up of two (or occasionally more) words to make a word or phrase with a meaning of its own. Usually a compound noun will consist of two nouns or a noun and an adjective. So, *compound noun* is itself a compound noun. They might end up as a single run-on word, two or more separate words, or a phrase separated by a hyphen. Rather unhelpfully, there are even fewer hard and fast rules on this than on most other aspects of English, so it is best to learn them as you go along.

Quiz 5

Can you match a word from column A with one from column B to form a compound noun? (Use each word only once.)

Column A	Column B
arm	stick
bull's	cleaning
bicycle	tree
cat	friend
chop	in-law
door	eye
dry	pit
finger	club
girl	seat
law	killer
lion	fiction
mother	boat
night	tamer
pain	burglar
passer	spotter
pear	print
pen	bell
science	by
train	suit
tug	knife

Counting Your Chickens:
Countable and Non-countable Nouns

Nouns can also be divided into *countable* or *non-countable* (or *mass*) nouns. Quite simply, if you can count the noun it's countable (e.g. horses or trees) and if you can't... well, you get it, don't you? Examples of non-countable nouns include water or literature. The key is can you ask the question 'how many?'

With non-countable nouns, we must talk in terms of general amounts, using adjectives known as quantifiers: *some, lots, not much* etc. We also use the adjective *less* in relation to non-countables, while we use *fewer* with countables.

Quiz 6

Identify whether the object is countable or non-countable.

1) Happiness
   Countable __ Non-countable __

2) Ball
   Countable __ Non-countable __

3) Distance
   Countable __ Non-countable __

4) Water
   Countable __ Non-countable __

5) Luggage
   Countable __ Non-countable __

6) Book
   Countable __ Non-countable __

7) Biscuit
   Countable __ Non-countable __

8) Flour
   Countable __ Non-countable __

9) Computer
   Countable __ Non-countable __

How Much?: Quantifiers

A *quantifier* is a word that tells us *how much there is* or *how many there are* of something. Numbers, of course, are quantifiers but there are many other words and phrases that give us a more general idea of amount or quantity. Some work only with countable nouns (e.g. *many, a few*), some with non-countable nouns (e.g. *a bit, not much*) and still others work with both (e.g. *enough, a lot of*).

Quiz 7

Choose which of the quantifiers suggested best finish the sentences that follow:

1) _____ people have problems with grammar.
   (a lot of / too much)

2) I think I got _____ questions right.
   (the majority of / not much)

3) I only drink _____ coffee because caffeine can give me a headache.
   (a little / a couple of)

4) With the deadline approaching, there was _____ time left.
   (some / not much)

Answers on page 180

5) Though _____ of the city was destroyed,
   _____ remained standing.
   (some / all / not much / a great deal)

6) He woke up with a headache, having drunk
   _____ wine last night.
   (too much / all)

7) He was sick after he ate _____ the cake.
   (all / a few of)

8) His essay was marked down for _____ attention
   to detail.
   (a lack of / little)

9) He had three tickets for the game so he took
   _____ friends.
   (a lot of / a couple of)

10) She catalogued _____ the library's books.
    (a little of / all)

Any Way You Look At It:
'Any', 'Some'

We use *some* in:
- positive sentences
  - e.g. I have some money.
- offers
  - e.g. Would you like some tea?
- questions anticipating a positive response
  - e.g. Could I have some dinner?

We use *any* in:
- negative sentences
  - e.g. I don't have any money.
- questions other than those described above
  - e.g. Do you need any help?

Other words based on the *any-* and *some-* stems (*anybody/somebody, anyone/someone, anything/something, anywhere/somewhere*) are governed by the same principles.

Quiz 8

With this in mind, mark the words that you think most appropriate to finish the following sentences.

1) I have _____ loose change in my pocket.
    (some / any)

Answers on page 181

2) We never go _____.
   (somewhere / anywhere)

3) I don't have _____ idea what to buy her for a gift.
   (some / any)

4) They don't know _____ in Canada.
   (somebody / anybody)

5) I know _____ who will be able to help.
   (someone / anyone)

6) Would you like to go _____ for the weekend if I pay for your ticket?
   (somewhere / anywhere)

7) 'I don't know _____,' the defendant cried out.
   (something / anything)

8) Is there _____ cheese in the fridge?
   (some / any)

9) Could you pour me _____ coffee?
   (some / any)

10) She knew _____ that she wasn't telling him.
    (something / anything)

The More the Merrier: Plurals

To make a singular noun plural, you just need to add an -s, right? Oh, if only it were that simple! Of course, many words do simply take an -s, (e.g. *book* becomes *books* and *dog* becomes *dogs*). However, there are exceptions. Loads of them:

- If a word already ends with:
  - an –s
  - or with an –x or –z sound
  - or a –ch or –sh
  - or with a –y preceded by a consonant

we normally add –es (and turn any spare –y into an –i).

- If a word ends with an –o (e.g. potato), we sometimes add an –es but not always (e.g. discos)
- If a word ends with –f or –fe (e.g. leaf or wife) – but not double –ff – we often take off these endings and replace them with -ves. At other times we simply add an –s (as with belief) while a few words can be pluralized either way (e.g. dwarf).

Quiz 9

Let's stop there for a moment to catch our breath. The cruel truth is that there are lots of rules about plurals but no strict rules to tell you when they come into play. This is an area where experience really is the best way to learn. Here is a list of words that can cause confusion. Have a go at turning them into plurals.

Singular	Plural
1) buffalo	
2) chief	
3) church	
4) cliff	
5) dish	
6) dress	
7) fax	
8) fish	
9) hoof	
10) key	
11) lady	
12) life	
13) proof	
14) scarf	
15) solo	
16) thief	
17) tomato	
18) torch	
19) waltz	
20) zoo	

Answers on page 181

Non-S-ential: More Irregular Plurals

There are plenty of other words that steer clear of –s endings altogether in their plural forms. Many of these words use endings derived from Latin, Greek and Old English. Others go for a change of vowel sounds instead. On the following page is a crossword to complete based on this distinctive set of words.

Quiz 10

Clues

Across

1 - Plural of cactus
6 - Plural of medium
7 - Singular of quizzes
8 - Plural of cod
9 - Singular of oxen
10 - Plural of die
11 - Plural of goose
15 - Plural of nucleus
16 - Singular of busses
17 - Plural of antenna

Down

2 - Plural of alumnus
3 - Plural of beau
4 - Plural of datum
5 – Alternative plural of person
9 - Plural of oasis
11 - Plural of genus
12 - Singular of nebulae
13 - Plural of fungus
14 - Plural of louse

Collecting Your Thoughts: Collective Nouns

A collective noun is used to describe a group of individuals. Examples include an audience, a class, an orchestra, a jury and a committee.

Quiz 11

Can you match the nouns from column A to the correct collective nouns in column B?

Column A	Column B
1) sailors	a) pack
2) singers	b) gaggle
3) ships	c) herd
4) flowers	d) library
5) sheep	e) fleet
6) geese	f) bouquet
7) books	g) school
8) fish	h) crew
9) wolves	i) flock
10) elephants	j) choir

Answers on page 182

A Conundrum of Quiz Questions: Unusual Collective Nouns

The animal kingdom in particular has some memorable examples of collective nouns. Here are fifteen that are particularly rich in imagery, but can you match the collective noun to the right species?

Quiz 12

Column A	Column B
1) cackle	a) apes
2) charm	b) lions
3) colony	c) crows
4) intrusion	d) moles
5) knot	e) hyenas
6) labour	f) jellyfish
7) murder	g) toads
8) parliament	h) finches
9) plague	i) dolphins
10) pod	j) tigers
11) pride	k) bats
12) shrewdness	l) ravens
13) smack	m) owls
14) streak	n) cockroaches
15) unkindness	o) locusts

All for One?:
Collective Nouns and Verb Agreement

In theory, since the collective noun treats a collection of individuals as a single entity, it should take the singular verb. However, sometimes we are referring to the actions of individuals within the group. In such cases, the noun takes the plural. Look at these examples:

- The family is coming for Christmas.
- The family were arguing throughout Christmas dinner.

In the first case, the family is being treated as a unit and so takes the singular. In the second instance, the family is being treated as a collection of individuals and so takes the plural.

Quiz 13

Decide which form of the verb should be used in the following sentences.

1) Many of the squadron _____ _____ in that battle.
                    (was lost / were lost)

2) The squadron _____ _____ all of its men in the attack.
                    (has lost / have lost)

3) The crowd _____ _____ as one.
                    (was singing / were singing)

4) The crowd _____ _____ amongst themselves.
(was fighting / were fighting)

5) The entire class _____ _____ the exam.
(was taking / were taking)

6) The class _____ _____ on several projects.
(was working / were working)

7) The staff _____ _____ signs of tension.
(was showing / were showing)

8) The whole staff _____ _____ out on strike.
(has walked / have walked)

9) The jury _____ _____ away to consider its verdict.
(was sent / were sent)

10) The jury _____ _____ to agree on a verdict.
(was unable / were unable)

Answers on page 183

42

Definitely maybe?:
A/An/The

An article is a word that helps us understand what sort of reference is being made to the noun that follows it. There are two main types of article –

- *A* or *an* are **indefinite articles** and indicate that we are talking about the noun in general terms.
- *The* is known as the **definite article** and generally indicates that we are talking about the noun in specific terms.

To understand the difference, consider the following two sentences:

- A car came down the road.
- The car came down the road.

In the first example, the indefinite article indicates that this might be any old car. In the second, however, the definite article shows that we are talking about one car in particular. Neither sentence is wrong but the example shows how important an '*a*' or '*the*' can be in establishing context.

Quiz 14

See how you get on with the following pairs of sentences. In each pair, one sentence takes the definite article and one the indefinite article.

1) I need to buy __ new pen.
2) Can you pass me __ pen next to you.
3) Pete is top scorer in __ school football team.
4) There were no spare seats on the bus as __ football team had got on at the previous stop.
5) London is __ wonderful city.
6) London is __ capital city of England.

A or an?

The basic rule says that you use *a* when you want the indefinite article in front of a word that begins with a consonant. If it starts with a vowel, use *an*. However, as if you needed to be told, there are a few exceptions.

- If a word begins with *h* (a consonant) that is sounded, as in 'house', then use *a*. If the *h* is silent, as in 'hour', use *an*.
- If a word starts with a vowel that is sounded like a consonant, use *an*. So, we talk about 'a European' because 'European' begins with a 'y' sound.

- Similarly, if a word starts with a consonant that is sounded like a vowel, use *an*. For instance, we refer to 'an MP' because the 'M' is sounded like a vowel (*em*). Though perhaps it shouldn't come as too great a surprise to find our MPs bending the rules!

Quiz 15

Now you're armed with this knowledge, have a go at filling in the gaps in the following passage.

1) We went to Paris last week for lunch. __ restaurant was fantastic.
2) It was next door to __ hotel where we stayed last year.
3) I had __ glass of wine and __ bowl of snails.
4) My friend had __ horse.
5) At first, our waiter brought us baguettes and Brie. It was __ honest mistake.
6) We took so long eating that we had to rush to get to __ station.
7) Then we got stuck in __ Channel Tunnel for __ hour and __ half.
8) When we got into London, it was so late that we decided to get __ taxi home.
9) I was so tired that I told my friend that I needed __ holiday.
10) 'Perhaps __ European tour by train,' my friend said.

Answers on page 184

The Place to Be:
'The' and Place Names

Often when we refer to a specific place, an article (definite or indefinite) is not necessary. For instance:

- 'He is going to London' *not* 'He is going to the London'.
- 'We are going to Trafalgar Square' *not* 'We are going to the Trafalgar Square'.

However, there are certain circumstances in which *the* is required. These include:

- for places with Republic, State or Kingdom as part of their name (e.g. the Czech Republic, the United States)
- for 'plural' names (e.g. the Philippines)
- with High Street (but not most other road names)
- for oceans, seas, rivers and canals
- for hotels, museums, theatres and cinemas
- for places containing an 'of' (e.g. the Tower of London)
- when describing a place in terms of the north / east / south / west of somewhere else

Quiz 16

Complete the following sentences by selecting the most appropriate form of the place name in each case.

1) I am going to _____ next week.
    (India / the India)

2) Have you been to _____?
    (Eiffel Tower / the Eiffel Tower)

3) Sherlock Holmes had rooms on _____.
    (Baker Street / the Baker Street)

4) We are going to _____.
    (Museum of Modern Art / the Museum of Modern Art)

5) It is sometimes said that you can see _____ from space.
    (Great Wall of China / the Great Wall of China)

6) The capital of Mongolia is _____.
    (Ulan Bator / the Ulan Bator)

7) The couple opened a dry-cleaners on _____.
    (High Street / the High Street)

8) There are some wonderful cheeses made in _____.
    (Netherlands / the Netherlands)

Answers on pages 184–5

9) We went from Buckingham Palace to _____.
(Westminster Abbey / the Westminster Abbey)

10) Laurence Olivier helped found _____.
(National Theatre / the National Theatre)

11) The plane landed at _____.
(London Heathrow Airport / the London Heathrow Airport)

12) The River Nile is longer than _____.
(Mississippi / the Mississippi)

13) We had fun pretending to prop up _____.
(Leaning Tower of Pisa / the Leaning Tower of Pisa)

14) The British sometimes refer to Australia and New Zealand as _____.
(Antipodes / the Antipodes)

15) There are some wonderful distilleries in _____.
(south of Ireland / the south of Ireland)

16) We love wine tasting in _____.
(southern France / the southern France)

From Me to You: Pronouns

If you are making several references to the same noun close together, your speech or writing will soon become very unwieldy if you repeat the noun every time. That is where *pronouns* come in. These are short and sharp words that take the place of nouns within a sentence. They come in three 'flavours' (or *cases* in technical-speak):

- nominative – when they replace a subject noun (e.g. *he*).
- accusative – when they replace an object noun (e.g. *him*).
- possessive – when they (appropriately enough) indicate possession. They replace a possessive adjective plus the following noun or noun phrase (e.g. *my car, your business*).

It's Personal: Personal Pronouns

Quiz 17

Let us begin by seeing if you can come up with all the basic personal pronouns. See how far you can get with the table below:

	Nominative	Accusative	Possessive
1st person singular	—	—	—
2nd person singular	—	—	—
3rd person singular	—, —, —	—, —, —	—, —, —
1st person plural	—	—	—
2nd person plural	—	—	—
3rd person plural	—	—	—

Quiz 18

In the following sentences there is some rather clunky repetition of nouns. Can you replace the bold typeface words and phrases with some suitable pronouns?

1) Toby's mother told **Toby** to do his homework.
2) Toby told **his mother** that he didn't want to do **his homework**.
3) The Greek government want the Elgin Marbles returned as they believe them to be **their Elgin Marbles**.
4) Claire went to see her boss, Jack, but **Jack** wasn't available to see **Claire**.
5) I wanted to buy my neighbour's car but I couldn't afford **my neighbour's car**.
6) Walter had a toy that he didn't want to share with his sister. 'It's **my toy**, it's not **your toy**,' he screamed.
7) My wife and I wanted to go on holiday so **my wife and I** went to the travel agency.
8) Our house is large so we invited all our friend to spend the weekend at **our house**.

Answers on page 185

Test Your Reflexives: Reflexive Pronouns

Reflexive pronouns are formed by adding –*self* to the singular forms and –*selves* to the plural forms of either the basic object pronoun (him, her, it, them) or the possessive adjective (my, your, our). They are used when the subject and object of a sentence are one and the same, the reflexive pronoun taking the place of the object (e.g. 'The careless barber cut *himself* with a pair of scissors'). Reflexive pronouns can also be used to add emphasis (e.g. 'I can't see the point of it, *myself*').

Quiz 19

Using each of the reflexive pronouns below only once, can you fill in the gaps in the sentences that follow.

herself — himself — itself — myself — ourselves — themselves — yourself — yourselves

1) You have to stop doing this to _____.
2) We treated _____ to dinner at the new restaurant in town.
3) She knew what she wanted for _____.
4) When you're away on holiday, be sure to look after _____.
5) The monkey was scratching _____ with a stick.
6) Count Dracula could not see _____ in the mirror.
7) They could not be trusted to behave _____.
8) I kicked _____ when I heard the correct answer.

Straight Back at You: Reciprocal Pronouns

There are two forms of reciprocal pronoun. *Each other* denotes a reciprocal relationship between two people or things, while *one another* is used for numbers greater than two.

Quiz 20

Put the correct reciprocal pronouns into the gaps in the following sentences.

1) You could tell that Allie and Fred loved _____ _____ just by being around them.

2) The group of children could not stop teasing _____ _____.

3) When they heard that the job had gone to someone else, the five interviewees commiserated with _____ _____.

4) After the competition ended in a draw, the two competitors congratulated _____ _____.

Answers on page 186

It's All Relative:
Relative Pronouns

The relative pronouns are *who*, *what*, *whom*, *that*, *whose* and *which*. Their job is to introduce subordinate clauses that give us further information about the noun that immediately precedes the relative pronoun (or, sometimes in the case of *which*, the whole of the preceding clause). People tend to interchange *which* and *that* at will these days but, strictly speaking, *which* should follow a comma and relate to a whole clause, while *that* covers the noun only and does not require a comma.

Quiz 21

The following sentences are missing their relative pronouns. Can you fill in the gaps?

1) Those _____ are blessed with beauty must avoid vanity.
2) The play _____ I directed was well received by the critics.
3) He juggled three flaming torches as he unicycled around the Big Top, _____ was something no one had ever done before.
4) The boy _____ feet were webbed was the best swimmer in the county.
5) The cab driver _____ took us to the airport didn't know the way.

Indefinitely Maybe:
Indefinite Pronouns

Indefinite pronouns come into their own when we do not wish to or are unable to refer to a specific noun.

Quiz 22

Below is a list of common indefinite pronouns. Use each only once to fill the gaps in the sentences that follow. And please note, it is very common to see even the most accomplished writers putting a hyphen in the middle of *no one*. Don't – it shouldn't be there.

all — any — anything — everyone — a few — no one — one — several — someone — something

1) In space, _____ can hear you scream.
2) Leave the chocolates alone; there are only _____ left.
3) I am sure I saw _____ up at the window.
4) Her best friend had dated _____ celebrities.
5) When questioned, the witness denied he had seen _____.
6) Have a look in the box. There's _____ for you.
7) What a great party. _____ had a wonderful time!
8) The good news called for champagne, but sadly they didn't have _____.
9) There were several thousand spectators and _____ had a good time.
10) I need a good lawyer. Do you know _____?

Answers on page 186

Who Cares?:
Interrogative Pronouns

Interrogative pronouns are used in place of nouns to ask certain questions. The list comprises *what, which, who, whose* and *whom* (with the option of adding the suffixes *-ever* and *–soever* if you so desire). Remember, *whom* is used when the *who* referred to is the object rather than the subject (e.g. to *whom* should I address this letter?) while *whose* is the possessive form of *who*.

Quiz 23

Got all that? As ever, the practice is rather more simple than the theory, so have a go at rewriting the eight statements that follow as questions using the most appropriate interrogative pronoun. For instance: 'This is his chair' would become '*Whose* chair is this?'

1) It is ten o'clock.
   (_____ _____ is it?)

2) I went to the school in the centre of town.
   (_____ _____ did you go to?)

3) Sir Christopher Wren designed this building.
   (_____ _____ this building?)

4) My profession is civil servant.
   (_____ _____ your profession?)

5) Kate is wearing her husband's t-shirt.
   (_____ _____ is Kate wearing?)

6) He voted for the Monster Raving Loony Party at the last election.

(_____ _____ _____ _____ _____ at the last election?)

7) I am going to drive my Porsche and leave my Micra at home.

(_____ _____ are you going to drive?)

8) Kerry borrowed the spare umbrella.

(_____ _____ the spare umbrella?)

Answers on page 187

Let Me Demonstrate:
Demonstrative Pronouns

The demonstrative pronouns – *this*, *that* (for singular nouns) and *these*, *those* (for nouns in the plural form) – serve to indicate something without actually naming it. *This* and *these* often signify nearness (in terms of space and/or time) while *that* and *those* refer to things further away.

Quiz 24

1) Where did you get the necklace you're wearing?
   (I got _____ at the market.)
2) What do you want me to do with the bags of clothes on the landing?
   (Take _____ to the charity shop.)
3) Why are you carrying all those jackets?
   (I'm taking _____ to the cleaners.)
4) What should I do with the book on the table over there?
   (Take _____ home with you and study it.)

Determined to Show You: Demonstrative Determiners

This, *that*, *these* and *those* can also be coupled with nouns, when they become *demonstrative determiners*.

Quiz 25

In this quiz, use the pictures to complete the sentences using suitable demonstrative determiners.

1) _____ _____ are all overdue.
2) Is _____ _____ free, please?
3) I live in _____ _____ on the hill.
4) Does my bum look big in _____ _____.
5) Are _____ _____ yours?
6) Do you know any of _____ _____?
7) Listen to _____ _____ singing.
8) How much is _____ _____ in the window?

Answers on page 187

Who's Who?:
Who, Who's, Whose and Whom

Many English-users experience difficulty in deciding when to use the various forms of *who*. Essentially, *who* is the subjective relative pronoun, *whom* is the objective form and *whose* is the possessive. A further element of confusion is added by *who's*, which is the contracted form of *who is*.

Quiz 26

These days, it seems that *who* has almost become acceptable both for the subject and the object but, old fashioned as it may be, we will make the distinction in this quiz. Simply choose which form of the word is the correct one to finish each sentence.

1) I don't know _____ to believe.
      (who / whom / whose / who's)

2) He admired George Washington, _____ was the first President of the United States of America.
      (who / whom / whose / who's)

3) Do you know _____ wallet this is?
      (who / whom / whose / who's)

4) I'm very grateful to Ken, _____ going to give me a lift to work.
      (who / whom / whose / who's)

Answers on page 187

5) _____ ate the last biscuit?
(who / whom / whose / who's)

6) _____ car are you going in?
(who / whom / whose / who's)

7) _____ going to come with me to the shops?
(who / whom / whose / who's)

8) To _____ should I address my letter?
(who / whom / whose / who's)

Answers on page 187

Branded for Life:
Proper Nouns That Became Common

Every now and again a brand name achieves such success or market dominance that its name becomes commonly accepted as the generic term for a product. Can you work out the brand names described here?

Quiz 27

1) Type of ballpoint pen
2) Clear sticky tape
3) Flying disc used as a toy
4) An item of women's underwear
5) Hook-and-loop fastening
6) Luxury recreational vehicle
7) Plastic storage containers
8) An outfit popular with circus performers and exercise fanatics
9) A type of raincoat
10) Self-adhesive notelets
11) Vacuum cleaner
12) Whirlpool bath associated with luxury

Answers on page 188

Verbal Dexterity: Regular Verbs

Most verbs in English are *regular*; that is to say they follow certain standard rules when they are conjugated. As a rule, you can conjugate a verb – that is, give its different forms according to voice, mood, tense, and so on – regardless of whom it refers to or what tense it is in if you know the verb's *infinitive* form (the most basic form of a verb, consisting of the verb preceded by *to*, and entirely unencumbered by *mood*, *person* or *tense*), the *past participle* form and the *present participle*. Take, for instance, the regular verbs *to mend*, *to dance* and *to live*:

infinitive	past participle	present participle
to mend	mended	mending
to dance	danced	dancing
to live	lived	living

Quiz 28

To ease you into the subject, can you complete the table below for the following regular verbs?

Infinitive	past participle	present participle
to allow		
to call		
to live		
to cry		
to study		
to sin		
to tie		
to develop		
to embarrass		
to meddle		
to race		
to nod		

To Be or Not to Be:
Common Irregular Verbs

It is indicative of the complexity of the English language that some of the most common of all verbs — *to be*, *to have*, *to do* and *to go* — are some of the most irregular. However, you have to master them if you want to master the language as a whole. See how you get on conjugating each of them.

Quiz 29

To be

	present	*past*
I		
you		
he/she/it		
we		
you		
they		

present participle	
past participle	

Answers on page 189

Quiz 30

To have

	present	**past**
I		
you		
he/she/it		
we		
you		
they		

present participle	
past participle	

Quiz 31

To do

	present	**past**
I		
you		
he/she/it		
we		
you		
they		

present participle	
past participle	

Answers on page 190

Quiz 32

To go

	present	**past**
I		
you		
he/she/it		
we		
you		
they		

present participle	
past participle	

Most Irregular: Irregular Verbs

Aside from those four key verbs, there are plenty of others that are irregular.

Quiz 33

In the list of irregular verbs below, you have the *infinitive* form but can you add the *simple past* and *past participles?*

infinitive	past simple	past participle
to arise		
to bear		
to become		
to begin		
to bite		
to blow		
to break		
to bring		
to burst		
to buy		
to choose		
to cut		
to do		
to draw		
to drive		
to eat		
to fall		
to feel		
to fly		

Answers on pages 190–1

infinitive	past simple	past participle
to forget		
to forsake		
to freeze		
to go		
to have		
to hide		
to know		
to lie		
to mistake		
to ride		
to ring		
to see		
to shake		
to sing		
to speak		
to steal		
to swear		
to swell		
to tear		
to throw		
to write		

Your Favourite Subject?: Subject and Object

A very basic sentence structure runs as follows: Subject – Verb – Object

In such a sentence, the subject tells us who or what is performing an action, the verb tells us what they are doing and the subject tells us whom or what is affected by the action.

Take, for instance, the following sentence: *'He writes poetry'. He* is the *subject* performing the action, which happens to be *writing*, while the *poetry* is what is affected by the action.

Quiz 34

In the following sentences, label the subject and object in each sentence.

1) He drove his car to the railway station.
   The subject is _____
   The object is _____

2) She ran her company efficiently.
   The subject is _____
   The object is _____

3) The locksmith cuts keys for a living.
   The subject is _____
   The object is _____

Answers on page 192

4) The rugby player scored a try.
   The subject is _____
   The object is _____

5) The soldier fired his gun at the target.
   The subject is _____
   The object is _____

Quiz 35

Often a sentence will also have an indirect object – that is to say, it tells us to whom or to what something is being done. In the following quiz, mark which of the three words listed under each sentence is the indirect object.

For instance, in *she took the jacket from him*, *him* is the indirect object, because *the jacket* is the direct object of *took*.

1) The teacher gave the students their homework back.
   (teacher ___ students ___ homework ___)
2) He paid her a compliment.
   (paid___ her___ compliment___)
3) The boss gave his secretary an hour to file the report.
   (secretary___ hour___ report___)
4) My wife made me dinner tonight.
   (me___ dinner___ tonight___)
5) Pete showed Anna his holiday photos.
   (Anna ___holiday___ photos___)

Any Object-ions?:
Transitive and Intransitive Verbs

Verbs can be classified as either transitive or intransitive. Despite sounding rather intimidating, the concept behind these words is really quite straightforward. Simply, a *transitive* verb has to have at least one *object* while an *intransitive* verb has *no object*. It is worth remembering that intransitive verbs will often be followed by an adverbial or prepositional phrase to add further information about the action described.

However, to keep you on your toes, quite a few verbs are both transitive and intransitive. To understand this better, consider the verb *to write*:

- I write.
- I write books.

Both sentences make perfect sense. In the first line there is no need for an object and so the verb is intransitive. In the second sentence, *books* is the object thus, the verb is transitive.

Quiz 36

In this first quiz, the verbs listed are all intransitive. Choose the correct one (you'll need to conjugate them) to complete each sentence:

collapse — go — sneeze — stay — weep

1) She _____ so hard that she almost fell over.
2) She _____ pitifully for hours.
3) I _____ to Canada.
4) The building _____ after the earthquake.
5) They _____ at the best hotel in town.

Quiz 37

Five of the ten sentences below contain transitive verbs and five contain intransitive verbs. Under each sentence, mark whether the verb is transitive or intransitive.

1) We arrived at the party an hour late.
   (Transitive __ Intransitive __)
2) He kicked the ball against the wall.
   (Transitive __ Intransitive __)
3) She lied about why her essay was not done.
   (Transitive __ Intransitive __)
4) It happens every fortnight.

(Transitive __ Intransitive __)

5) She is running a half-marathon on Sunday.
   (Transitive __ Intransitive __)

6) You have been taking photos all day.
   (Transitive __ Intransitive __)

7) You buy a new computer game every week.
   (Transitive __ Intransitive __)

8) You have waited quite long enough.
   (Transitive __ Intransitive __)

9) The old lady died, aged 102.
   (Transitive __ Intransitive __)

10) I lost my favourite pen.
    (Transitive __ Intransitive __)

Do As You Would Be Done To: Transitive and Intransitive Verbs

Transitive verbs can be expressed in one of two *voices*: the *active* or the *passive*. In an active sentence, the *subject* is *doing*. In a passive sentence, the *subject* is *done to* (intriguingly, this sometimes means that a transitive verb doesn't need a traditional object, as the subject becomes the object). Confused? Have a look at the following football-related examples:

● Brazil beat Argentina. (*Active*)
● Argentina were beaten by Brazil. (*Long passive*)
● Argentina were beaten. (*Short passive*)

Answers on page 193

Quiz 38

Read the following sentences and decide which voice the verb is in.

1) You were seen at the theatre.
   (active _____ passive _____)
2) You watched a play at the theatre.
   (active _____ passive _____)
3) The man was chased down the street.
   (active _____ passive _____)
4) The mugger ran away.
   (active _____ passive _____)
5) We are going to paint the living room.
   (active _____ passive _____)
6) The colour was chosen by me.
   (active _____ passive _____)
7) The doctor was visited by the old man.
   (active _____ passive _____)
8) The old man had a nasty cough.
   (active _____ passive _____)

Quiz 39

In this exercise, rewrite each sentence, converting them from the active to the passive voice (as in the following example).

- I baked the bread. (*Active*)
- The bread was baked by me. (*Passive*)

1) The waiter served dinner.
2) Fred drove the car.
3) The defender scored a penalty.
4) William Shakespeare wrote *Romeo and Juliet*.
5) Laura wore the green dress.
6) Mr Wilson teaches my class.
7) Uncle Arthur trains those racing pigeons.
8) We will eat the birthday cake tomorrow.
9) A child painted that picture.
10) Tommy copied my homework.

Answers on page 193

Verbal Tension

Tenses can be a source of tension, so let's see how on top of them you are. At the most basic level, tenses are very simple and hugely useful, as they tell us when an action being described is happening. In broad terms, this will be at one of three times: in the past, in the present or in the future. However, there are actually twelve tenses (some experts argue there are even more but a dozen seems quite enough for now). They subtly give us detail as to when exactly the action described is occurring and if the action is quickly over and done with or on-going.

Below, the verb *to study* has been conjugated into the twelve tenses, which I hope will help with some of the quizzes that follow. (For the difference between shall and will, see page 87.)

I study	Present Simple
I am studying	Present Continuous
I have studied	Present Perfect
I have been studying	Present Perfect Continuous
I studied	Simple Past
I used to study	Imperfect
I was studying	Past Continuous
I had studied	Past Perfect (or Pluperfect)
I will study	Future
I shall/will be studying	Future Continuous
I shall/will have studied	Future Perfect
I shall/will have been studying	Future Perfect Continuous

What are You Doing?: Conjugating for Beginners

The following quick quizzes are designed to see how good you are at forming the basic tenses. Take the verb at the end of the sentence, conjugate it and write the correct form in the space provided.

Quiz 40

A) Present Simple

I _____ fish and chips.(**eat**)

He _____ to the cinema.(**go**)

They _____ a café.(**run**)

You _____ to work.(**walk**)

B) Present Continuous

I _____ Japanese.(**learn**)

He _____ to music.(**listen**)

You _____ a movie.(**watch**)

They _____.(**fight**)

C) Present Perfect

We _____ to Lisbon.(**go**)

You _____ the Great Barrier Reef.(**see**)

I _____ a novel.(**write**)

They _____ a house.(**buy**)

D) Present Perfect Continuous

I _____ round the park.(**run**)

You _____ lectures.(**miss**)

They _____ every day.(**surf**)

It _____ for a month.(**break**)

Answers on pages 194–5

E) Simple Past

I _____ into town.(**walk**)

You _____ some new shoes.(**choose**)

He _____ his wallet.(**lose**)

We _____ tennis.(**play**)

F) Past Continuous

You _____ your car.(**drive**)

They _____ a mountain.(**climb**)

We _____ in a helicopter.(**fly**)

She _____ a dress.(**design**)

G) Imperfect

We _____ parties every week.(**throw**)

I _____ watercolours.(**paint**)

You _____ in Brussels.(**work**)

They _____ my school.(**attend**)

H) Past Perfect

I _____ the bill at the restaurant.(**pay**)

It _____ off the shelf.(**fall**)

They _____ their car.(**sell**)

You _____ for a big present.(**ask**)

I) Future

I _____ you at the cinema.(**meet**)

You _____ your favourite scarf.(**wear**)

It _____ tomorrow.(**rain**)

We _____ the lottery this weekend!(**win**)

J) Future Continuous

I _____ in Italy next year.(**study**)

You _____ with your family at Christmas.(**stay**)

We _____ at the Savoy on Tuesday.(**dine**)

He _____ the country this time next year! (**run**)

K) Future Perfect Continuous

I _____ at university for five years by the time I graduate.(**be**)

The clock _____ in that corner for a hundred years next year.(**stand**)

You _____ that chicken for two hours soon! (**cook**)

We _____ for five years in October.(**marry**)

L) Future Perfect

I _____ my degree by next summer.(**complete**)

You _____ an Oscar by the time you're thirty.(**win**)

We _____ in five countries when we move to Australia.(**live**)

They _____ the cup five times if they beat their opponents in the big match.(**lift**)

Answers on pages 194–5

No Time Like the Present:
The Present Tense

Quiz 41

Below are some sentences that should be in the present tense. Choose the more appropriate of each of the two options to complete the sentences.

1) Dave _____ *The Great Gatsby* by F. Scott Fitzgerald at school this term.
    (is reading / reads)
2) He _____ his novel for the last week.
    (is reading / has been reading)
3) She _____ reading every night before bed.
    (has enjoyed / enjoys)
4) She _____ reading all her life.
    (is loving / has loved)

All Present and Correct

Quiz 42

In the exercise below, you need to fill in the gaps. In each case, we have indicated which tense the missing verb should be. You need to choose the most appropriate verb from the list provided (using each only once) and then conjugate it. Simple as that!

be — eat — have — lecture — look — love — miss — read — run — see — tell — tour — tuck — visit — wish — write

A Postcard from New York

Dear Pam and Bob,

Well, we _____ (**present continuous**) the most wonderful time in New York. Our hotel _____ (**present simple**) wonderful and the staff _____ (**present simple**) around after us. They _____ (**present perfect continuous**) us about all the best places to visit. We _____ (**present perfect**) in some wonderful restaurants. Stan _____ (**present continuous**) into a huge hamburger as I _____ (**present simple**) this note!

Today we _____ (**present continuous**) round the city on a bus. We _____ (**present perfect**) Central Park and the Museum of Modern Art. I _____ (**present perfect continuous**) the guidebook you lent us so I _____ (**present simple**) Stan about all the places we _____ (**present continuous**).

Answers on page 196

My, how I _____ (**present simple**) this city. We _____ (**present simple**) that you were here and _____ (**present continuous**) forward to seeing you very soon.

_____ (**present continuous**) you both,

Beryl and Stan xx

What's Past Is Past: The Past Tense

Quiz 43

Choose the correct form of the past tense to complete the gaps in the following sentences which should then make sense as a full piece.

1) Janet _____ the London Marathon last May.
   (used to run / ran)
2) Janet _____ the marathon for the third year in a row.
   (had run / was running)
3) Janet _____ at the thought of running such a distance.
   (used to shudder / has been shuddering)
4) Janet _____ to beat her record but missed it by ten seconds.
   (used to hope / had hoped)

All in the Past

Quiz 44

In the exercise on page 86, you need to fill in the gaps. In each case, we have indicated which tense each missing verb should be. You should now choose the most appropriate verb from the list provided (using each only once) and then conjugate it.

be – bring – choose – dream – enjoy – entertain – fight –
greet – kill – leave – lock – open – rain – say – take – train –
triumph – walk – want – watch – wrestle

Answers on page 197

THE ROME BUGLE
Ides of March, AD 182
From our special correspondent at the Empire Games

Yesterday _____ (**past simple**) the opening day of the Games at the Colosseum and an expectant crowd _____ (**past simple**) the Emperor Commodus ecstatically. The crowd _____ (**simple past passive**) by a packed programme of contests and when the spectators left, they _____ (**past continuous**) more.

Early in the morning the heavens _____ (**past perfect**) so spectators _____ (**simple past**) shelter beneath the stadium's vast awning. 'It _____ (**past continuous**) for at least three hours,' one crowd-member told me. 'But we _____ (**past perfect**) ourselves still. My own father _____ (**imperfect**) how the Games always _____ (**imperfect**) the rain!'

As has become the custom, in the first bout after lunch, brave Commodus himself _____ (**simple past**) a prisoner-of-war who _____ (**past perfect passive**) especially for the honour. The two men _____ (**past continuous**) in fierce combat for many minutes before the Emperor at last _____ (**simple past**). The prisoner _____ (**past continuous passive, negative**) as a gesture of the Emperor's mercy.

It is said that the Emperor _____ (**past perfect**) a fierce tiger in preparation for the match. He was quoted as saying, 'When I was a boy, I _____ (**imperfect**) the gladiators and always _____ (**simple past**) of being one. I have worked hard all my life to stay fit and strong. These last six weeks I _____ (**past continuous**) especially hard for my match today. I _____ (**simple past**) into the arena this afternoon full of confidence and I _____ (**simple past**) it the victor.'

The Future's Bright: The Future Tense

Quiz 45

Choose the correct form of the future tense to complete the gaps in the following sentences.

1) Max _____ his driving test next month.
   (will have been taking / will be taking)
2) He _____ at the examination centre at 9 a.m. on Friday the 4th.
   (will arrive / will have been arriving)
3) He _____ to drive for six months.
   (will learn / will have been learning)
4) He _____ 24 lessons by the time of the test.
   (will be having / will have had)

It Shall Be Done: Shall and Will

Shall and *will* are often used interchangeably but there are differences in sense between the two words, and quite useful those differences are too. Traditionally, *shall* is used for the first person and *will* for the second and third persons.

Shall used with the first person singular or plural expresses a simple statement of fact:

Answers on page 197

- I shall see you tomorrow at 10 a.m.

Used with the second or third person singular or plural, it implies a command, promise or strong assertion:

- You shall regret this.

Note, also, the difference between shall and will in questions:

- Shall I make some tea? (i.e. Would you like me to make some tea?)
- Will I make some tea? (i.e. Am I going to make some tea?)

Quiz 46

Have a look at the following questions and decide whether each gap requires the word *shall* or *will*?

1) You _____ do as you're told.
2) Cinderella _____ go to the ball.
3) They promised they _____ reimburse me fully.
4) I _____ pick you up in the morning.
5) They _____ go for a ride on the London Eye during their holiday.
6) _____ I pass my exams?
7) _____ I get your coat for you?

Future Proof

Quiz 47

In the exercise below, you should fill in the gaps. In each case, we have indicated which tense each missing verb should be. You need to choose the most appropriate verb from the list provided (using each only once) and then conjugate it.

carry — complete — continue — eat — fulfil — launch — leave — lose — retire — return — search — stay — travel — work

NASA PRESS RELEASE

20 September 2025

Tomorrow NASA _____ (**future**) its first manned vessel to Mars. The team of three astronauts _____ (**future continuous**) for several months and, after docking, _____ (**future**) on the planet for five days. By the time they land, each astronaut _____ (**future perfect**) 500 dehydrated meals and _____ (**future perfect**) up to a stone in weight.

The mission leader, Capt. Dwight Starblaze, _____ (**future continuous**) out a series of experiments to discover if there is life on the Red Planet. He _____ (**future continuous**) a time capsule full of artefacts from Earth for alien life-forms to discover. By the end of the trip, Capt. Starblaze _____ (**future perfect**) his forty-second trip outside of the Earth's atmosphere.

Answers on page 198

Capt. Starblaze told journalists: 'By the end of this mission, I
_____ (**future perfect continuous**) on space missions for
over twenty years. I have told my wife that, once I'm back on
Earth, I _____ (**future**) as I _____ (**future perfect**) all
my childhood dreams. I must pay credit too to the members of
my team, who _____ (**future**) the good work of NASA: Stella
Burst, who herself _____ (**future perfect continuous**) for
Martian life for ten years by the time we return; and Kirk Moondust,
who _____ (**future**) to complete a PhD in Martianology
next year.'

Answers on page 198

Small But Perfectly Formed: Auxiliary Verbs

Auxiliary verbs are those verbs which help to establish the tense, mood or voice of other verbs. There are three primary auxiliaries (*am, have* and *do*). Note, these three can all work as stand-alone verbs (e.g. I **am** a teacher) as well as with other verb forms (e.g. I **am** thinking). The other auxiliary verbs (*can, could, may, might, must, ought (to), shall, should, will, would*) require a main verb to make real sense.

Quiz 48

In each of the following sentences, can you identify the auxiliary verbs?

1) The doctor will see you tomorrow.
2) I couldn't believe my eyes.
3) The dog had been waiting an hour for his walk.
4) I have eaten too much.
5) He ought to take his driving test soon.
6) We should have been going on holiday today but it was cancelled.
7) You do paint beautifully.
8) They must have caught the last bus home.
9) I might try to buy a new house.
10) I am going to the cinema.
11) Who would have thought it was possible?
12) I can't be blamed for that.

Answers on page 199

In the Mood:
Verb Moods

There are three main moods in English that help us to understand the context of a verb:

- Indicative – when the verb is expressing a statement of fact or asking a question (e.g. I **have** two eyes, **Are** you ready?).
- Imperative – used in commands (e.g. **Get** in here now!).
- Subjunctive – indicating an unreality or a hypothetical state. That is to say, the action hasn't happened or doesn't exist (e.g. If I **were** ten years younger...)

Quiz 49

Read the following sentences and decide which mood each verb in bold is in.

1) Don't **drink** that poison!
2) I wouldn't do that if I **were** you.
3) Thomas Hardy **was** a novelist.
4) **Show** me the money!
5) Canberra **is** the capital of Australia.
6) Have you **seen** the Sistine Chapel?
7) If I **were living** by the beach, I would surf every day.

If I May...:
The Subjunctive

Guaranteed to strike fear into the average grammar student, the subjunctive is not as bad as all that. Perhaps we feel so uncertain around it because it is designed to deal with uncertain situations – suppositions, hopes, desires, imaginings, doubts and suggestions. Often the subjunctive is signposted by the word *if* and also by *may... be....*

- The present subjunctive form differs from the regular present indicative in the third person singular only, where the *−s* is omitted at the end of the word. For example:
  - She **goes** clubbing. (indicative)
  - He suggested that she **go** clubbing with him. (subjunctive)
- The past subjunctive is exactly the same as the regular past indicative.
- With the verb *to be*, use *be* for all persons for the present subjunctive and *were* for the past subjunctive. For example:
  - We request you **be** here tomorrow.
  - He wished he **were** taller.
- For all verbs, the future subjunctive is formed by *were* + the infinitive for all persons.
  - If **I were to run** the marathon tomorrow, I would collapse.

Quiz 50

Let's see how much of that has sunk in. Can you work out the correct subjunctive form of the verb provided to complete these sentences?

1) May the force _____ with you! (be)
2) He proposed that she _____ his half of the business. (buy)
3) If we _____ our own restaurant, who would look after the kids? (run)
4) If I _____ that job, I would have to work long hours. (take)
5) She wished that she _____ slimmer so she could buy those new jeans. (be)
6) She suggests she _____ a table for next Saturday. (book)
7) Would you take the job if you _____ me? (be)

On One Condition: The Conditional

Conditionals are sentence structures that deal with a possible or imaginary situation, rather than an actual one. They have one of two basic structures:

- If something happens, something else happens.
- Something happens, if something else happens.

There are four types of conditionals:

- The zero conditional, which describes a certainty at any time.
    - If you heat butter, it melts.
- The first conditional, which describes a likely proposition looking into the future.
    - If I eat that whole cake, I shall be sick.
- The second conditional, which describes either an unlikely proposition looking into the future or an impossible proposition in the present.
    - If I found a million pounds, I would buy a castle in Italy.
    - If I had two heads, I would wear two hats.
- The third conditional, which describes something happening in the past different to what actually happened.
    - If I had seen the lit cigarette, I would have stopped the fire.

Quiz 51

In the quiz below, tick which type of conditional you think each of the sentences is.

1) If I had known she would be at the party, I wouldn't have gone.
   (Zero conditional ___ First conditional ___ Second conditional ___ Third conditional ___)

2) If you eat garlic, your breath smells.
   (Zero conditional ___ First conditional ___ Second conditional ___ Third conditional ___)

Answers on page 200

3) If I train hard, I will get fit.
(Zero conditional ___ First conditional ___ Second conditional ___ Third conditional ___)

4) If she studies hard, she will pass her exams.
(Zero conditional ___ First conditional ___ Second conditional ___ Third conditional ___)

5) If they had seen the hotel, they would never have booked a room there.
(Zero conditional ___ First conditional ___ Second conditional ___ Third conditional ___)

6) If I had the time, I would paint great artworks.
(Zero conditional ___ First conditional ___ Second conditional ___ Third conditional ___)

7) If you go out in the rain, you get wet.
(Zero conditional ___ First conditional ___ Second conditional ___ Third conditional ___)

8) If I invented a time-machine, I would travel to Tudor times.
(Zero conditional ___ First conditional ___ Second conditional ___ Third conditional ___)

Answers on page 200

Get Not-ed!:
Negatives

To form most basic negatives, we insert *not* after an auxiliary verb:

- I am not running
- I do not run
- I have not run
- I cannot run (note, cannot is one word) etc.

In the absence of an auxiliary word, default to *do* (in the appropriate tense) + *not* + the infinitive minus *to*. For instance:

- She visited the cinema.
- She **did not** visit the cinema.

There are a few further rules to bear in mind:

- If *be* is the main verb, *not* follows *be*. For instance:
    o I am the king.
    o I **am not** the king.
- If *have* is the main verb, *do not* precedes have. For instance:
    o You have a million pounds.
    o You **do not have** a million pounds.
- *Not* comes before infinitives and present participles. For instance:
    o It is foolish **not to be prepared**.
    o The audience stared at the comedian, **not laughing**.

Quiz 52

Now it's your turn. Rewrite the following sentences to make the bold typeface verbs negative.

1) It is dangerous to **drive** slowly
2) I **want** to be unpopular.
3) I **am** as rich as King Midas.
4) My time machine is **working**.
5) With the headmaster's words ringing in her ears, she set off down the corridor, **running**.
6) I am too cautious to **pay** my insurance premium.
7) I have **met** them before.
8) I **have** a fleet of private aeroplanes.
9) He **proposed** to her on a hill overlooking Florence.
10) I **do** my French homework each weekend.

Answers on page 200

A Big No-No!

You may remember from your school maths lessons that if you multiply two negative numbers together, you get a positive. Grammar works in much the same way. Yet even the most powerful and influential can get confused on this point. Take former US President George W. Bush, who once noted: 'How can you possibly have an international agreement that's effective unless countries like China and India are not full participants?'

Quiz 53

Can you correct the following sentences to eliminate the double negative and achieve the meaning that is clearly intended but badly executed in the original?

1) I didn't do nothing!
2) There isn't nowhere I'd rather be than here with you.
3) I have not never been late for college all term.
4) There's not nothing I don't know.
5) I haven't been out nowhere all night.
6) There's not no one who will do the job better than me.

Answers on page 200

Under Contract:
Contractions

If you want to be a little less formal, *not* formulations may also be contracted and may take different forms depending on the conjugation. So, *cannot* can be rendered as *can't* or *couldn't*, *do not* as *doesn't*, *don't* or *didn't*, *have not* as *hasn't*, *haven't* or *hadn't* and *be not* as *isn't*, *aren't* or *wasn't*. Most other auxiliary verbs can also take '*n't*', with the exceptions of *shall* and *will* (which become *shan't* and *won't*, respectively).

This has particular repercussions for the word order of questions formed with negatives:

- Using the full form, the word order is:
    - Auxiliary verb + subject + not e.g. 'Should we not see if he's all right?'
- Using the contracted form, the word order is:
    - Auxiliary verb + n't + subject, e.g. 'Shouldn't we see if he's all right?'

Quiz 54

Rewrite the following sentences to form negative questions, using both the full and the contracted forms:

1) We must go.

a) _____

_____

b) _____

_____

2) You would like to try the wine.

a) _____

_____

b) _____

_____

3) You have seen enough.

a) _____

_____

b) _____

_____

4) They should go there.

a) _____

_____

b) _____

_____

5) It is warm outside.

a) _____

_____

b) _____

_____

Answers on page 201

Part and Parcel:
Participles

Participles are the forms of verbs used with auxiliary verbs. On their own they lack person, tense, voice, mood and number.

The present participle, which is used in all continuous tenses, can be found by taking the present continuous tense of a verb and knocking off the auxiliary *to be*. Present participles almost always end with *–ing*.

For instance:

- Present continuous -> I am running
- Present participle -> running

The past participle usually, though not always, has one of the following endings: *-ed*, *-d*, *-t*, *-en* and *–n*. It can be identified by taking the past perfect tense and knocking off the auxiliary verb *to have*. For instance:

- Past perfect -> I had looked
- Past participle -> looked

Participles can also serve as adjectives. For instance, we talk about *running water* or *boiled potatoes*.

Quiz 55

Read the following sentences and insert appropriate participles formed from the verbs in the list provided (using each only once).

be — bore — burn — bring — confuse — cover — destroy — direct — invest — open — sadden — smell — speak — surprise

1) Wonderfully _____ by Luc Besson, the film was a triumph.
2) _____ wisely, your money can give you a good return.
3) _____ his door, he was hit with a snowball.
4) _____ new to the company, he was keen to make a good impression.
5) The drink got him in the end, _____ his liver.
6) The ancient city was lost to history, _____ by tons of sand.
7) The lecturer droned on, _____ the students.
8) _____ by the news, she shed a tear.
9) The signs were covered up, _____ the tourists.
10) _____ by the size of the present, he almost fell off his chair.
11) _____ the roses, the gardener thought how much he loved his job.
12) They opened the bottle of wine _____ by their friends from France.
13) There was nothing left of the photograph, _____ in the flames.
14) They listened to the announcements, _____ by the station manager.

Answers on page 201

Ing-comprehensible:
Gerunds

Gerunds or verbal nouns are formed by adding *–ing* to a verb to create a noun. Now, it may have occurred to you that a verb with an *–ing* on the end might also be a participle. As usual, it's all about context. Is the *–ing* word acting as part of a verb (and is therefore a participle), as an adjective (and so is what is called an adjectival participle) or as a noun (and is therefore a gerund)? Consider the following examples:

- Dancing is a good way to keep fit. (*Dancing* is the subject of the sentence and so is a gerund).
- I saw her on the dance-floor, dancing to her heart's content. (*Dancing* is the verb associated with the noun *her* and is therefore a participle).
- He was a boring teacher. (*Boring* is describing the teacher, serving as an adjective and, therefore, is an adjectival participle).

Quiz 56

Look at each of the following sentences and then indicate whether the highlighted word is a gerund or a participle.

1) **Rushing** around the place, I soon grew tired.
   (gerund ___ participle ___)
2) He liked nothing more than **baking** cakes.
   (gerund ___ participle ___)
3) **Swimming** is a wonderful skill to have.
   (gerund ___ participle ___)

4) **Beginning** today, I am going to give up smoking.

   (gerund ___ participle ___)

5) Beginning today, I am going to give up **smoking**.

   (gerund ___ participle ___)

6) **Defying** her parents, the teenager went to the all-night party.

   (gerund ___ participle ___)

7) **Passing** his exam was a great boost to his confidence,

   (gerund ___ participle ___)

8) **Breaking** the speed limit is not advised.

   (gerund ___ participle ___)

9) You will get lost if you are **reading** your map wrongly.

   (gerund ___ participle ___)

10) His favourite pastime was **fishing** for trout.

    (gerund ___ participle ___)

11) My uncle is **writing** poetry.

    (gerund ___ participle ___)

12) I enjoy **writing** poetry.

    (gerund ___ participle ___)

Make Your Mark:
Punctuation

Punctuation marks provide us with the clues we need to understand how a piece of written language is structured and also help us to interpret meaning. Without them, we would become submerged in a sea of letters and numbers, strung together without any sort of framework and virtually unintelligible. That may have been fine for James Joyce but for the rest of us it simply won't do.

Quiz 57

Below are the symbols for ten of the most common punctuation marks, their names and their definitions. Can you match up each of the three columns in the correct order?

Symbol	Name	Definition
.	quotation mark	denotes either possession or the contraction of two words (when it is used in place of the omitted letter or letters).
?	semicolon	denotes the end of a standard sentence.
!	dash	denotes direct speech.
—	question mark	denotes that the following text summarizes or explains the preceding part of the sentence.
-	comma	used either to break a long word at the end of a line of text or to link two words together.
"	hyphen	denotes a pause or a separate clause within a sentence.
:	exclamation mark	used either alone or as one of a pair (in place of parentheses) to introduce an aside, an interruption or a new piece of information, to indicate a sudden change in emotion or thought, or to show the omission of words.
;	apostrophe	denotes a direct question.
,	full stop	used to join two or more independent clauses that don't really deserve to be sentences in themselves.
'	colon	an alternative to the full stop used to grab the reader's attention or to indicate strong emotion.

Quiz 58

Here are some sentences in need of punctuation. Decide which symbol is the most appropriate.

1) Fire Run for your lives
2) It was so cold that I had to wear my hat gloves and scarf
3) Give me data demanded Sherlock Holmes
4) Do you know the way to Amarillo
5) You cant make a silk purse out of a sows ear
6) It came to him suddenly in the bath Eureka
7) Moscow is the capital city of Russia
8) She had to pay a large fine on her long overdue library book
9) It was the best of times it was the worst of times
10) He liked his new job title Head of Client Relations

Stream of Consciousness: Difficult Punctuation

Quiz 59

James Joyce was notorious for writing complex sentences with little punctuation to guide the reader. Here is a short paragraph related to him. Can you punctuate it to make it readable?

Have you read much James Joyce I enjoyed *Dubliners* particularly you could understand what he was talking about because he employed commas full stops question marks and even apostrophes thats not the case in *Finnegans Wake* which was a book I couldnt get on with my friend loves *Ulysses* most he told me once its the best book I have ever read

Answers on page 203

Dreaded Apostrophe's:
The Apostrophe

Look at an average pub menu board or a sign in a grocer's shop window and there's a good chance that you'll find an example of gross misuse of the apostrophe. It sometimes seems that such abuse of punctuation can only be the result of wilful intent on behalf of the author. The truth, though, is that many people are just utterly confused as to what they should do with the funny, little floating symbol that turns up seemingly randomly.

So let's briefly recap the basic rules:

- Use an apostrophe to replace a letter/letters removed from a contracted word or phrase.
  - e.g. You cannot forget the apostrophe in can't!
- Use an apostrophe to indicate the possessive (before the 's' in a singular noun, after the 's' in a plural and not at all with pronouns).
  - e.g. In Britain, the Prime **Minister's** home is at 10 Downing Street.
  - There he will host a regular cabinet **ministers'** meeting.
  - It is not **his** favourite part of the job.

Quiz 60

Look at the following sentences and decide whether each apostrophe is being employed correctly or not.

- a) The dog span round, chasing it's own tail.
  (Correct ___   Incorrect ___)

- b) Its not the end of the world to misplace an apostrophe but it shouldn't happen too often!
  (Correct ___   Incorrect ___)

- c) The road is so slippery that I daren't drive my car.
  (Correct ___   Incorrect ___)

- d) I am going to stay at Tom's and Claire's new house at the weekend.
  (Correct ___   Incorrect ___)

- e) The banana's my favourite fruit. What is more, banana's only cost a few pence each.
  (Correct ___   Incorrect ___)

- f) Our rugby team were the winners of the County Schools' Championship.
  (Correct ___   Incorrect ___)

- g) Free pizza's for all diners who arrive before 7pm.
  (Correct ___   Incorrect ___)

- h) I love Greek drama. Sophocles' plays are my favourites.
  (Correct ___   Incorrect ___)

Answers on pages 203–4

Quiz 61

Here is some wording on an advertising board from the local high street, written by someone who has not quite mastered the art of the apostrophe. You'll need to get rid of some and add a few others but Sid and Joe would be most grateful for your editorial help!

Great Deal's at Sid's and Joe's Fruit and Veg Shop!

Its price-slashing madness so don't miss out!

Orange's – 50 pence for three.
Fresh pineapple juice – fall in love with it's taste!
Spanish tomatoes' – your favourite and mine'!
Jersey Royal potatoes – they're perfect for the summer!
Yummy strawberry puddings' – ideal for children's' parties!

Are these the High Streets best deals? Too right. (Much cheaper than John's Farm Foods!)

**Only two children at a time and no dog's!
(For more special deals, visit our stall at St Barnabus's Market this Saturday too. You shant regret it.)**

Comma Chameleon: The Comma

There is perhaps no more humble symbol in written English than the comma, yet it has the ability to bring sense where nonsense threatens to reign. Sit back and be amazed at all the places where we employ the comma:

- where you wish a reader to pause
- after introductory words or phrases that come before a main clause
- between separate clauses within a sentence
- before direct speech
- in addresses and place names where one part of the place name furnishes information about the other
- around non-restrictive phrases
- after items in a list
- in large numbers, after every third digit (reading from right to left)
- before and after an appositive (that's a word or phrase that defines or modifies a noun or pronoun that precedes it)
- after a dependent clause that comes before an independent one
- after consecutive adjectives
- before certain conjunctions linking independent clauses
- in place of a deliberately omitted word under certain circumstances
- before *too* when it is used in the sense of *also*
- to emphasize certain adverbs
- after greetings and sign-offs in letters

Note, too, the American inclination towards the Oxford or serial (or Harvard) comma, which puts a comma before the final *and*, *or* or *nor* in a list of two or more elements. In Britain, the Oxford comma is generally avoided unless it is considered to do away with ambiguity in a particular scenario.

Quiz 62

Having established the power of our little friend the comma, it is now your turn to attempt to add commas in the right places in the following sentences.

1) After going out for a night on the town I was very sick.
2) His brother attended Keble College Oxford.
3) I walked through the haunted house trembling and was almost in tears by the time I found the exit.
4) We've got an early start tomorrow so let's get some sleep.
5) Give it a rest will you?
6) Millie the Dog won first prize in her class and was best in show too.
7) Yours sincerely Frank Hobbs
8) The hotel was crumbling the staff rude.
9) In 1666 the Great Fire of London broke out in Pudding Lane.
10) His favourite bands of all time were The Beatles The Rolling Stones The Who and The Spice Girls.
11) In 1940 with Hitler rampaging through Europe Winston Churchill became Prime Minister.
12) When I was ten years old in 1986 Diego Maradona led Argentina to the World Cup.
13) Barak Obama the President of the United States of America was born in Hawaii.
14) Bagpuss was an old fat furry catpuss.
15) The judge asked 'How do you plead?'
16) There are approximately 60000000 people living in the UK.

Don't Quote Me: Quotation Marks

Quotation marks (or 'inverted commas') have several uses. They can indicate direct speech, quotations or titles of short publications, and sometimes they are used to imply irony (e.g. 'The trouble with "do-gooders" is that they end up doing more harm than good.').

The problem is, while most of English grammar has fairly definite rules (even if they are at times bewildering), quotation marks don't (and there is much disagreement between those in the UK and the USA to boot).

For a start, should quotation marks be single or double? Take your pick, though for our purposes let's plump for single for primary quotes and double for any further material to be quoted within a quotation.

Quiz 63

There are other moot points too complex to embark on here (such as the question of whether punctuation at the end of a sentence should be inside or outside of the inverted commas). However, in each of the following sentences, there is an error that is so wrong it is beyond debate. Can you spot them and rewrite the sentence correctly?

1) Give me that! 'she demanded rudely'.
2) 'I do like it here, he said quietly.'
3) He told me that he was 'fed up with his grammar homework'.
4) He said, I want to climb 'Mount Everest.'
5) She said 'she was sorry' for the trouble she'd caused.
6) 'Don't cry,' she said. You'll soon feel better.
7) He reported, 'I heard her whisper don't leave now in his ear.'

Answers on page 205

Dash It All:
Hyphenation

As well as breaking up long words too long to fit at the end of a line, a hyphen is used between words to signify their particularly close relationship, especially when joining two words to form a single modifier (e.g. *She was a fresh-faced girl.*). Yet hyphenation in the modern age is something of a hit and miss business. Or, rather, a hit-and-miss business.

Over time, words that were once routinely hyphenated (such as *week-end*) have merged into single words (*weekend*). Elsewhere, we happily cope with the omission of hyphens from words that should have them, as long as we can discern the true meaning of a phrase. For instance, technically we should describe a particularly heavy truck as a *ten-ton truck*. However, if we are told that *he was hit by a ten ton truck*, there is little room for confusion and we can forgive the omission of the hyphen.

Sometimes, though, such an omission heralds complete confusion. Take the following examples:

- Dave had 200-odd friends on Facebook.
- Dave had 200 odd friends on Facebook.

In the first example, it is clear that Dave has around 200 Facebook friends. In the second example, we might well understand it to mean that he has 200 friends who are odd. Such cases go to show that the hyphen can be an invaluable weapon in your grammatical armoury.

Quiz 64

In the following exercise, tick which sentence in each pair you think is correctly hyphenated.

1) We live in a fifth-floor flat.
   We live in a fifth floor flat.

2) We live on the fifth-floor.
   We live on the fifth floor.

3) I felt let-down by the producers.
   I felt let down by the producers.

4) After all the excitement beforehand, the show was a complete let-down.
   After all the excitement beforehand, the show was a complete let down.

5) She noticed a thick layer of dust round-the-clock.
   She noticed a thick layer of dust round the clock.

6) The politician was not a fan of round-the-clock news.
   The politician was not a fan of round the clock news.

7) I enjoyed a glass of 20-year-old Scotch.
   I enjoyed a glass of 20 year old Scotch.

8) The Scotch is 20-years-old.
   The Scotch is 20 years old.

9) He bowls with his left-hand.
   He bowls with his left hand.

10) He was the best left-handed cricketer I ever saw.
    He was the best left handed cricketer I ever saw.

11) He was caught in a twelve-mile traffic jam.
    He was caught in a twelve mile traffic jam.

12) The traffic jam stretched back for twelve-miles.
    The traffic jam stretched back for twelve miles.

13) We are going away for two weeks.
    We are going away for two-weeks.

14) We are going on a two-week holiday.
    We are going on a two week holiday.

Answers on pages 205–6

Paint Me a Picture: Adjectives

Adjectives are those words that describe nouns and pronouns. They tell us, for instance, how big something is, what it looks like, where it's from, how many there are and countless other characteristics.

Quiz 65

Using each only once, choose the most likely adjective from those listed here to complete the sentences that follow.

blue — bumpy — elegant — greasy — jolly — lazy — numerous — nutritious — proud — round — short — sparkling — thundering — vast — wooden

1) Coco was a _____ clown.
2) Her dress was very _____.
3) She enjoyed the occasional glass of _____ wine.
4) The sea was the most inviting _____.
5) The motorcyclist was going to jump across the _____ canyon.
6) The _____ dog slept all day.
7) His favourite breakfast was a _____ fry-up.
8) The father-of-the-bride was very _____.
9) He struggled to get the square peg into a _____ hole.
10) The landing at the airport was very _____.
11) The headmaster addressed the pupils in a _____ voice.
12) The 6' model refused to date _____ men.
13) The athlete tucked into a _____ bowl of salad.
14) The little boy loved his _____ train set.
15) The film star had _____ gentlemen friends.

Answers on page 206

All in a Name:
Adjectives from Proper Nouns

Some adjectives are derived from proper nouns to describe, for instance, historical periods, artistic styles, nationality, geographical locations and philosophical outlooks.

Quiz 66

From the clues below, can you work out the adjectives?

1) Relating to a Victorian novelist whose characters include Abel Magwitch and Bill Sykes.
2) Relating to the author of *The 95 Theses* and a leading figure of the Reformation.
3) Relating to the Prague-born writer of *The Metamorphosis*.
4) Relating to the German operatic composer of the *Ring Cycle*.
5) Relating to the reign of England's Virgin Queen.
6) Relating to the Latin-American culture, especially that found in the United States of America.
7) Relating to the most famous creation of Miguel de Cervantes and used to describe someone who is idealistic to the point of impracticality.
8) Relating to a race of ancient gods and once used as the name of a famous passenger liner.

How Are You Doing That?: Adverbs

Adverbs are words we use to add further meaning to verbs, adjectives and other adverbs. They help answer questions such as *how, when, where, how much* and *how often?* They often end with *–ly* (e.g. *carefully*) but by no means always (e.g. *hard, fast*). Nor are all words ending in *–ly* adverbs (e.g. *family*)!

Quiz 67

In the quiz below, choose the most appropriate verb and an accompanying adverb from the lists provided (using each word only once) to fill the gaps in the sentences.

VERBS

accused — addressed — applauded — approached — crept —
gave — laughed — paraded — played — rained — ran — slept —
spoke — stared — waited

ADVERBS

bravely — enthusiastically — fast — heartily — heavily —
longingly — nervously — nicely — patiently — peacefully — rudely —
silently — truthfully — victoriously — wrongly

1) It _____ _____, which was good for the garden.
2) The cat _____ up _____ on the mouse.
3) The children _____ together _____.
4) The policeman _____ the innocent man _____.
5) The old man _____ _____ at the rude joke.
6) The woman _____ _____ for the doctor.
7) The audience _____ _____ after the great show.
8) The cup-winning team _____ _____.

Answers on pages 206–7

9) The dog _____ _____ in his bed.
10) The sprinter _____ _____ in the Olympic final.
11) The explorer _____ the lion _____.
12) The boy _____ the teacher his homework _____, fearing he had got it all wrong.
13) The teenager _____ at the beautiful girl next door _____.
14) The lawyer _____ the jury _____.
15) The man _____ to the waiter _____.

Neither One Nor the Other

Remember, some words can act as both adverb and adjective! In the quiz below, is the word in **bold** an adverb or an adjective?

Quiz 68

1a) I love the sound of bird song in the **early** morning.
    (adverb __   adjective __)
1b) I get up **early** to listen to the birds.
    (adverb __   adjective __)
2a) Tom worked **hard** before the exam.
    (adverb __   adjective __)
2b) The exam was **hard.**
    (adverb __   adjective __)
3a) Sue likes **fast** cars.
    (adverb __   adjective __)
3b) Sue drives **fast**.
    adverb __   adjective __

4a) Pistol Pete would not give the judge a **straight** answer.

(adverb __   adjective __)

4b) The judge sent him **straight** to jail.

(adverb __   adjective __)

5a) I got the **late** bus home.

(adverb __   adjective __)

5b) I arrived home **late**.

(adverb __   adjective __)

6a) The aeroplane was flying **low**.

(adverb __   adjective __)

6b) It was **low** on fuel.

(adverb __   adjective __)

Shall I Compare Thee...: Comparatives

Comparatives are adjectives or adverbs that are used to compare two things – that is to say, one thing is described as more or less like another. So, for instance, we might note that an African elephant has **larger** ears **than** an Indian elephant, or that Wayne Rooney is **less** beautiful **than** Scarlett Johansson (sorry, Wayne, but it's true and, besides, I'm sure you're the better footballer...).

To form a regular comparative, you can often simply add *–er* to the end of an adjective or adverb. So, *loud* for instance becomes *louder*. However, there are many exceptions to this rule (especially if the adjective or adverb becomes rather too much of a mouthful with an *–er* at the end), so we sometimes simply add *more* before the adjective or adverb. For instance, *handsome* becomes *more handsome*.

Whenever we want to say something is lesser, we always just add *less* before the adjective or adverb. Of course, there are some more oddities too. Take *good*, for instance, which becomes *better*.

Answers on page 207

Quiz 69

Here are ten sentences in need of a comparative. Choose the most suitable word from the list provided and put it into its comparative form.

a lot — bad — cheap — clever — cute — far — fast — fat — noisy — smelly

1) The lecturer was smart but his colleague was _____.
2) Uncle Fred weighs a lot but Aunt Edna is _____.
3) The little boy was loud but his sister was _____.
4) Baked beans don't cost much but caviar is _____.
5) Australia is a long way away but New Zealand is _____.
6) Having a cold is bad but having 'flu is _____.
7) Alan Sugar has a lot of money but Lakshmi Mittal has _____.
8) Carl Lewis was speedy but Usain Bolt runs _____.
9) The kitten looks sweet but the puppy is _____.
10) Stilton is stinky but your socks are _____.

Super-Dooper: Superlatives

The *superlative* allows us to describe our subject as imbued with a certain characteristic to the greatest possible degree – or at least to a greater degree than the things it is being compared to. In other words, while a comparative compares only a few things, a superlative is the best or greatest of three or more. The regular formulation requires us to add *–est* to the end of the relevant adjective or adverb. So, for instance, *loud* becomes *loudest*. But just as with comparatives, we avoid making words too long. *Handsome* thus becomes *most handsome* (or perhaps *least handsome*). Meanwhile, beware of irregular examples, such as *bad*, which becomes *worst*.

Quiz 70

The ten sentences below are crying out for superlatives. Once again, choose the most suitable word from the list provided and put it into its superlative form.

famous — far — feared — good — long — populous — prolific — small — tall — valuable

1) Mount Everest is the _____ mountain in the world.
2) Platinum is the _____ metal.
3) Lionel Messi is the _____ footballer in the world.
4) The Vatican City is the _____ country in the world.
5) The Mona Lisa is the _____ painting in the world.
6) Neptune is the _____ planet from the Sun.
7) The Nile is the _____ river in the world.
8) Tokyo is the _____ city in the world.
9) Milton was the _____ poet of his age.
10) Jack the Ripper was the _____ criminal of the Victorian age.

Answers on page 208

All In Order: The Order of Adjectives

Depending on how flowery you want your descriptions to be, you can keep on adding adjectives to your heart's content. However, certain combinations of adjectives sound plain wrong if presented out of order. While we might happily request a *nice, hot cup of tea*, if we ask instead for a *hot, nice cup of tea*, it just sounds strange.

In fact, though by no means written in stone, there are useful guidelines as to where to position particular types of adjectives (starting with most distant from the modified noun):

- Position 1: Opinion
- Position 2: Size
- Position 3: Age
- Position 4: Shape
- Position 5: Colour
- Position 6: Material
- Position 7: Origin
- Position 8: Purpose

Quiz 71

With this in mind, can you arrange the adjectives attached to the following sentences in the most logical order?

1) He was having dinner with a _____, _____ woman.
   (Adjectives: *beautiful, young*)

2) She was particularly interested in acquiring the masterworks of _____, _____ watercolourists.
   (Adjectives: *French, old*)

3) She specifically requested that he buy the _____
_____ cream.
(Adjectives: *Jersey, pouring*)

4) There were a dozen _____, _____, _____
bottles sitting behind the bar.
(Adjectives: *blue, glass, large*)

5) He was delighted with the _____, _____,
_____, _____ shoes he'd bought.
(Adjectives: *golden, running, size-10, stylish*)

6) She always carried around a _____, _____,
_____, _____, _____ bag.
(Adjectives: *big, hessian, knitting, old, puce*)

7) The child was fascinated by an _____, _____,
_____, _____, _____ cuckoo clock.
(Adjectives: *green, impressive, 19th-century, Swiss-made,
wooden*)

8) They lay on a bed covered in the _____, _____,
_____, _____, _____, _____,
_____ sheet available.
(Adjectives: *brand new, cotton, finest, large, square, valance,
white*)

Answers on page 208

Intensely Testing: Intensifiers

Intensifiers are words that can be used to give greater impact to an adverb, adjective or verb. Probably the most common intensifier is *very*. To be sad is one thing, but to be very sad is quite another.

Quiz 72

In the quiz below, choose the most appropriate intensifier to complete each sentence.

1) Bill was _____ ill for a week after the operation. (dangerously / easily)
2) Africa is a _____ bigger continent than Europe. (absolutely / much)
3) John was _____ hurt when he crashed his car. (highly / seriously)
4) That was _____ the best first date Kate had ever been on. (easily / extremely)
5) Deep sea diving on your own is _____ dangerous. (bitterly / extremely)
6) Sandra is a _____ accomplished pianist. (much / highly)
7) Winning the lottery was an _____ amazing feeling. (absolutely / highly)
8) I was _____ upset when I heard the bad news. (easily / really)
9) Jan is an _____ gifted opera singer. (absolutely / exceptionally)
10) A Siberian winter is _____ cold. (much / bitterly)

My, Oh My!: Possessive Adjectives

Possessive adjectives (not to be mixed up with possessive pronouns) are useful little words that tell us to whom the noun in question belongs.

Quiz 73

Using each only once, complete the following sentences with the possessive adjectives listed.

his — her — its — my — our — their — your

1) The tigers defended _____ territory ferociously.
2) _____ neighbours invited us round for a barbecue.
3) It's _____ party and I'll cry if I want to!
4) He was very proud of _____ efforts.
5) Emily enjoyed the way everyone admired _____ new hat.
6) _____ new job is just perfect for you!
7) The cat leapt in the air when it saw _____ own reflection.

Answers on page 209

Shall I Compare Thee...: Similes and Metaphors

Similes and metaphors are ways of comparing two things with similar characteristics and offer the opportunity to make your prose sound rather fancy and poetic. The difference is that a simile says something is *like* something else; a metaphor says something *is* something else (even though it isn't).

Quiz 74

To ease you in, can you spot which of the following are similes and which are metaphors?

1) She was grinning like the cat that got the cream.
2) He is a man-mountain.
3) He is as cunning as a fox.
4) The cars crunched into each other as if someone had let off a rifle.
5) He is a greyhound on the racetrack.

Metaphorically Speaking: Metaphors

Quiz 75

In this quiz, can you partner up the two halves of the sentences to achieve suitable metaphors?

1)	The killer had	a)	a silver dollar suspended in the sky.
2)	It was raining	b)	he is a veritable encyclopaedia.
3)	His legs had turned	c)	my rock.
4)	The Moon was like a	d)	he's a pig.
5)	He is so reliable, he is	e)	that was a mirror glass.
6)	I was shocked she married	f)	he was a sheep.
7)	At the dinner table,	g)	a heart of stone.
8)	I looked at myself staring back from the lake	h)	to jelly.
9)	He followed her round unthinkingly;	i)	a snake like him.
10)	He knows so much;	j)	cats and dogs.

Answers on page 210

Likeability: Similes

Quiz 76

Here are some of the most famous literary similes of all time. Can you match up the beginnings (numbered 1 to 10) and ends (opposite) of the sentences correctly and so avoid rewriting literary history?

1) 'Holmes looked at him thoughtfully like...
   (*The Casebook of Sherlock Holmes* by Sir Arthur Conan Doyle)

2) 'O my love is like...
   (by Robert Burns)

3) 'Her hair was rich as...
   (*Cider with Rosie* by Laurie Lee)

4) 'Why, man, he doth bestride the narrow world like...
   (*Julius Caesar* by William Shakespeare)

5) 'The very mist on the Essex marshes was like...
   (*Heart of Darkness* by Joseph Conrad)

6) 'The very mystery of him excited her curiosity like...
   (*Gone with the Wind* by Margaret Mitchell)

7) 'Elderly American ladies leaning on their canes listed toward me like...
   (*Lolita* by Vladimir Nabokov)

8) 'The late afternoon sky bloomed in the window for a moment like...
   (*The Great Gatsby* by F. Scott Fitzgerald)

9) 'The other was fair, as fair as can be, with great masses of golden hair and eyes like...
   (*Dracula* by Bram Stoker)

10) 'It was not really a happy question to ask him; it was like...
    (*Peter Pan* by J. M. Barrie)

a)   ... the blue honey of the Mediterranean.'

b)   ... a Colossus.'

c)   ... a master chess-player who meditates his crowning move.'

d)   ... pale sapphires.'

e)   ... a door that had neither lock nor key.'

f)   ... a wild bee's nest and her eyes were full of stings.'

g)   ... a gauzy and radiant fabric.'

h)   ... a red, red rose'

i)   ... an examination paper that asks grammar, when what you want to be asked is Kings of England.'

j)   ... towers of Pisa.'

Answers on page 210

And Another Thing:
Conjunctions

Conjunctions are words or short phrases that allow us to connect two words, phrases, clauses or sentences together. There are four main categories of conjunctions:

- coordinating conjunctions – used to join two sentences (or parts of sentences) of equal importance. You can use the following mnemonic to remember them: FANBOYS (for, and, nor, but, or, yet, so).
- subordinating conjunctions – used to link a main clause to a subordinate clause (e.g. because, although).
- compound conjunctions – short phrases usually ending in as or that (e.g. *as long as...* and *so that...*).
- correlative conjunctions – used in conjunction with other conjunctions (e.g. *either... or...* and *not only... but also...*)

Quiz 77

In this quiz, choose the more appropriate conjunction from those suggested and use it to rewrite the following lines as complete sentences. All the conjunctions in this quiz come from the first three sub-categories described above.

1) He had got an A in his A-level maths / he was only ten years old.
(even though / provided that)

2) The teacher looked fierce / she was really very kind.
(but / and)

3) He got sent to prison / he robbed an old lady.
   (because / if)

4) She was rich and famous / still she wasn't happy.
   (yet / because)

5) She was very tall / slim.
   (and / while)

6) He went to Paris / he could visit the Eiffel Tower.
   (so that / as soon as)

7) She left the night club / the bouncers threw her out.
   (before / so that)

8) He wanted to be sure the picture was genuine / he was
   going to pay so much for it.
   (if / provided that)

9) She would go to the concert / she could get a lift.
   (provided that / before)

10) He will stop taking the medicine / he feels better.
    (as soon as / while)

11) Heels repaired / you wait.
    (while / as soon as)

12) She has not worked as hard / she came back from her
    holiday.
    (since / while)

Answers on page 211

Choice Language:
Either/Or

Quiz 78

This quiz tests you on correlative conjunctions. Simply match the correct sentence opening to the appropriate ending. Either you'll get them right... or you won't.

Openings

1) **Both** Terry
2) **Either** Charlie
3) **Neither** Russia
4) I am going on holiday **whether** you go
5) He **not only** drove the car

Endings

a) **nor** the Netherlands have ever won the soccer world cup.
b) **and** Chris applied for the same job.
c) **or** Bill will give you a lift to the show.
d) **but also** built it from scratch.
e) **or** not.

The Preposition Proposition:
Prepositions

Prepositions are those words that help locate a noun or pronoun in time or space. Does that all sound a little *Doctor Who*? In reality, prepositions are the little words that often slip past us almost unnoticed. For instance, among the league of prepositions we may count the following words: *on, at, over, before, after, by* and *in*.

Time For a Quiz:
Temporal Prepositions

Quiz 79

Let's start with the prepositions that locate their subjects in time. Take a look at Dave's diary for the week, then in the statements that follow replace the blanks with suitable prepositions.

Dave's Diary:

Monday 20 June
Pub with Bill (first pint for a month!)

Tuesday 21 June
Gym 7-9pm

Wednesday 22 June
Cinema with Jill 8pm

Thursday 23 June

Friday 24 June
Breakfast meeting with Jack
Lunch meeting with Gerald

Saturday 25 June
Football 3pm
Kelly's birthday 7pm

Sunday 26 June
6am - Fly to Thailand!

The Statements

1) Dave's off to the pub tonight. Dave has not drunk alcohol _____ 20 May.
2) He will be at the gym _____ 7pm _____ 9pm tomorrow.
3) He has tickets for a film _____ 8 pm _____ Wednesday evening.
4) He must remember to turn his phone off _____ the movie.
5) Dave doesn't have a free evening _____ Thursday.
6) He will meet Jack _____ Friday _____ going to meet Gerald.
7) He is going to Kelly's party _____ football.
8) Dave must give his front door keys to his neighbour _____ he goes on holiday. The neighbour has agreed to water Dave's plants _____ he gets back.

Space Cadets:
Spatial Prepositions

Quiz 80

This quiz tests your knowledge of the prepositions that locate their subjects in space. Using each of the prepositions listed only once, complete the story of Jessica the Cat.

by – in – on – to – through – under – over – behind – inside – upon

1) Jessica the Cat was sitting _____ the window.
2) She spied a bird flying _____ the sky.
3) The bird landed _____ the lawn.
4) Jessica walked _____ the door and crawled _____ the cat flap.
5) She slunk _____ a bush.
6) She leapt _____ a wall.
7) She crept silently until she was just _____ the bird.
8) A moment later there was a bird _____ Jessica's belly and a cat with a big grin _____ her face.

Answers on page 212

I Sentence You....:
Sentence Structure

A sentence, as if you didn't know, is a sequence of words that can stand alone to make a statement, ask a question or give a command. It comprises the following elements:

- a capital letter at the start.
- a subject and a predicate (the predicate being the other main part of a sentence that includes the verb and any objects or phrases governed by the verb). A 'sentence' without both subject and verb, which relies on the context of other sentences to convey its meaning, is known as a *fragment*.
- a full stop, question mark or exclamation mark at the end.

Quiz 81

In this quiz, simply mark the part of each sentence that is the predicate.

1) Global warming is a worrying phenomenon.
2) Beijing is a very interesting city.
3) Nestled in the branches of the tree was a raven.
4) Tomorrow we are going to the cinema.
5) Waiting outside the shop was the old man's dog.
6) The blood-red rose was the glory of his garden.

Don't Get a Complex:
Types of Sentence

There are four major classifications of sentence structure, related to the number of clauses contained therein. A clause, by the way, is a distinct part of a sentence containing a subject and its finite verb. So here are the four types:

- the simple sentence, consisting of a single clause (e.g. 'I am studying grammar.').
- the compound sentence, consisting of two or more independent clauses, usually joined together by a coordinating conjunction (e.g. 'I am studying grammar but he is studying maths.').
- complex sentences, which have main clauses and subordinate clauses (e.g. 'Although it is complicated, I am getting better at grammar.'). Note, in the example in parenthesis, *I am getting better at grammar* is the main clause as it can stand alone, while *Although it is complicated* is the subordinate clause because it cannot stand alone.
- compound-complex sentences, consisting of multiple clauses (e.g. 'In trying to explain the different types of sentence structure, I have had to resort to an explanation, which you are reading now, that is full of clauses, both main and subordinate, that begins to render the whole passage, which is growing increasingly long, difficult to read and, as I am sure you will agree, a little unwieldy.')

Quiz 82

Setting aside compound-complex sentences for a moment (not least for reasons of space), see if you can correctly identify whether each of the following sentences is simple, complex or compound.

1) We are intending to cruise in the Norwegian fjords next year.
   (simple___ compound___ complex___)

2) She did not buy those new shoes, even though she thought they were beautiful.
   (simple___ compound___ complex___)

3) We have won the Cup for the last two years and we plan to win it again this year.
   (simple___ compound___ complex___)

4) All of our friends are married with children.
   (simple___ compound___ complex___)

5) They were going to a wedding at the weekend so Beatrice went to buy a new outfit.
   (simple___ compound___ complex___)

6) Having agreed to pick up the kids, I missed the end of the movie.
   (simple___ compound___ complex___)

7) I am hoping to get to the party but Louise cannot make it.
   (simple___ compound___ complex___)

Answers on page 212

8) Because of bad weather, the game was abandoned.
   (simple___ compound___ complex___)

9) After we finished our main course, we asked the waiter for the dessert menu.
   (simple___ compound___ complex___)

Relatively Speaking: Relative Clauses

Clauses introduced by a relative pronoun are called, logically enough, relative clauses. These subdivide into two further categories:

- restrictive clauses, which define something in the main clause and are essential for full comprehension of the sentence.
  - The games **that we played as children** have stayed with me into old age.
- non-restrictive clauses, which add extra information but are not essential.
  - The tall man, **who had red hair**, was convicted of the theft.

Answers on page 212

Quiz 83

Read the following lines and decide if the highlighted clause is restrictive or non-restrictive.

1) Cats, **which are a natural enemy of mice**, hunt silently.
   (restrictive clause ___ non-restrictive clause ___)
2) The man **who finds an alternative to fossil fuels** will be very rich.
   (restrictive clause ___ non-restrictive clause ___)
3) The present **that you gave me** is just wonderful.
   (restrictive clause ___ non-restrictive clause ___)
4) Your gift, **which is just perfect**, has pride of place on my mantelpiece.
   (restrictive clause ___ non-restrictive clause ___)
5) The woman **whom we asked** did not know the answer.
   (restrictive clause ___ non-restrictive clause ___)
6) The woman, **whose dog was utterly adorable**, showed us the way to the park.
   (restrictive clause ___ non-restrictive clause ___)

Answers on page 213

Are We All in Agreement?: Agreement Between Noun and Verb

A subject noun and its verb should always agree, which is to say that if the noun is in the singular so should the verb be, while a plural noun goes with the plural form of the verb. Most of the time this is quite straightforward:

- **I am** getting to grips with grammar.
- **We are** getting to grips with grammar.

However, now and again things get more complex. Here are a few more general rules to keep in mind:

- If two nouns are joined by the conjunction *and*, the verb should go in the plural.
  - 'My friend **and** I **are** going to the football.'
- A conjugation implying the subjects are not doing the same thing accompanies a verb in the singular.
  - 'Do you know if Jack **or** Jill *is* going up the hill?'
- *Either/or* and *neither/nor* constructions demand the singular.
- *Anybody, anyone, everybody, everyone, somebody, someone, each, every* and *one* all take the singular.
- *A few, both,* and *several* always take the plural.
- *All, any, most* and *some* take the singular if used in conjunction with non-countable nouns but take the plural with countable nouns.
- Numerical expressions (such as collective nouns) can take either the singular or the plural, depending on whether the noun is being thought of as a single unit or as a collection of individuals (see pages 39–42).
- An intervening subordinate clause does not affect the verb.
  - 'My wife, as well as my daughter, **is** travelling in Australia.'

Quiz 84

That is quite enough rules for now. Time to put them into action. Choose the correct word to finish each sentence.

1) Claire and Alison _____ two of the keenest dancers I know.
(is / are)

2) Our dog _____ a great entertainer.
(is / are)

3) Either Pete or Gordon _____ going to help you with your bags.
(is / are)

4) When I was growing up, both of my next-door neighbours _____ exceedingly kind.
(was / were)

5) Neither my mother nor my father _____ a very good swimmer.
(was / were)

6) I don't know anybody who _____ better at Scrabble than my Gran.
(is / are)

7) Everybody in the class _____ got a pass in the exam.
(has / have)

8) Several of my colleagues _____ tickets for the big concert.
(has / have)

9) Some cars _____ more fuel-efficient than others.
(is / are)

10) Some verse _____ difficult to read.
(is / are)

11) Fifty pounds _____ too much to pay for a dinner.
(is /are)

12) His rock band _____ being signed to a major label.
(is /are)

13) His team _____ going their separate ways at the end of the season.
(is /are)

14) Everyone in his school, as well as in all the other schools in the borough, _____ invited to perform at the arts festival.
(was / were)

Just in Case:
Agreement in Case

Subjects, objects and verbs should agree with each other in case as well as in number. This tends only to be a real problem when we get into the realm of the pronoun, when an apparent object might actually be a subject. Here are the major points of confusion:

- Is there a 'missing' verb or are there other 'missing' words? If so, in some cases the pronoun should be in the nominative case, even though this sometimes feels counter-intuitive. For instance we should say *He is wiser than I* rather than *He is wiser than me*. This is because what we are really saying is *He is wiser than I am*.

- However, some hidden verbs do take an object. For instance, we would say *I admire her almost as much as him* because what we are really saying is *I admire her almost as much as I admire him*.

- If the personal pronoun follows *but*, it should be in the case it would have been in if the hidden verb were not hidden. For instance, we might say *I waited five*

Answers on page 213

hours in the rain for tickets to Wimbledon. Who but I? What we really mean is Who but I would wait?

It is worth remembering that in the modern world, we readily overlook some inaccurate agreement, especially in speech. However, not in this quiz!

Quiz 85

Armed with all that above, see if you can correctly complete the following sentences:

1) He hit _____ during our boxing bout.
   (I / me)

2) You are much cleverer than _____.
   (he / him)

3) I like him far less than _____.
   (she / her)

4) I managed to make a cup of 'coffee' using gravy granules!
   Who else other than _____?
   (I / me)

5) That really is not for _____ to say.
   (I / me)

6) I am a great fan of _____.
   (they / them)

Answers on page 213

How Can I Phrase This: Phrases

A phrase is any group of words (it might contain two words or many more) that are not constructed round a verb but which act together as a single unit in terms of meaning and grammar.

There are five main types of phrase:
- noun phrase – assumes the role of a noun, as subject, direct object or the object of a preposition.
- verb phrase – any group of words containing a verb but not a subject.
- adjectival phrase – acts like an adjective to qualify, or modify, a noun.
- adverbial phrase – acts like an adverb to qualify, or modify, a verb.
- prepositional phrase – consisting of a preposition plus a noun or noun phrase.

Looks complicated? Well, perhaps a little, but in practice it's easier than you might think to spot them. And once you can identify phrases, you'll have a much greater understanding of how sentences are constructed.

Quiz 86

Take a look at the sentences below and try to work out what sort of phrases are in italics.

1)   I saw the Queen **at Buckingham Palace**.

_____

2)   **Almost every home** has a television.

_____

Answers on page 214

3) He could run a mile ***more quickly than most***.

    _____

4) I saw the man ***screaming like a baby***.

    _____

5) She is ***as pretty as*** a picture.

    _____

6) He ate his dinner ***like a pig at the trough***.

7) He enjoyed reading his ***book about the First World War***.

    _____

8) She dreamed of a pot of gold ***at the end of the rainbow***.

    _____

9) The kitten ***played with a ball of wool***.

    _____

10) They were a ***really friendly*** crowd.

    _____

11) King Kong ***liked to climb skyscrapers***.

    _____

12) He got promoted ***quite unexpectedly***.

    _____

13) He found a ten pound note ***down the side of the sofa***.

    _____

14) ***Most of my friends*** are richer than I am.

    _____

15) The naughty child ***felt thoroughly ashamed of himself***.

    _____

16) ***The King of Zaire*** has many wives.

    _____

17) His favourite view was ***across Loch Ness***.

    _____

18) I stood next to an ***exceptionally tall*** man.

    _____

19) I am hoping to go on holiday ***in the near future***.

    _____

20) My six-year-old nephew is ***cleverer than*** I am.

    _____

Answers on page 214

Don't Leave Them Dangling: Misplaced Modifiers

A modifier describing a noun should be placed as close as possible to its related noun to avoid confusion or ambiguity. Consider the following two sentences:

- The girl was walking her dog *in a short skirt*.
- The girl *in a short skirt* was walking her dog.

The first statement suggests there was a dog in a short skirt being taken for a walk. This, presumably, was not the intended meaning. This is a classic example of a **misplaced modifier**. Rather, the girl taking the dog for a walk is wearing a short skirt, as expressed clearly in the second statement.

This sort of confusion is particularly common where there are **dangling** (or **misrelated**) **participles**:

- Running for the bus, the new shop caught Pete's eye.
- Running for the bus, Pete's eye was caught by the new shop.

In the first statement, we seemingly have a *new shop* running for the bus (the shop is the subject of the main clause and, therefore, we assume it to be the subject of the participle too). This being ludicrous, we must assume that, in fact, Pete was running for the bus, as is accurately depicted in the second statement.

Quiz 87

Choose the less ambiguous sentence in each of the following pairs.

1) a) He killed a lion wearing slippers and pyjamas.
    b) Wearing slippers and pyjamas, he killed a lion.

2) a) Jack still regularly attends the church where he was married.
    b) Jack still attends the church where he was married regularly.

3) a) I began to pick up the cushions scattered around the living room.
    b) Scattered around the living room, I began to pick up the cushions.

4) a) He was standing next to a cafe wearing a denim jacket and shades.
    b) Wearing a denim jacket and shades, he was standing next to a cafe.

5) a) While climbing a tree, the ladder gave way.
    b) While I was climbing a tree, the ladder gave way.

6) a) Standing on the balcony, we had a breathtaking view of the mountains.
    b) Standing on the balcony, the view of the mountains was breath-taking.

7) a) The mother of the convicted man said at a press conference
       outside the court that God would judge her son.
    b) The mother of the convicted man said that God would
       judge her son at a press conference outside the court.

8) a) The greengrocer sold apples to his customers wrapped in
       cling film.
    b) The greengrocer sold apples wrapped in cling film to
       his customers.

That is the Question:
Question Words

Quiz 88

In this test, can you rearrange the following statements to turn
them into questions? There is no need to add any additional words.

1) That chair is free.
2) He was late for his appointment.
3) Bob can't go to the show.
4) You have got a big house.
5) The post has arrived.

Answers on pages 214–15

Quiz 89

Next, can you complete the following exchange by writing the questions that would elicit the responses provided. Use each of the question words listed only once. You even get some key vocabulary to help you phrase your questions.

Are? — Does? — How many? — How much? — What? — When? — Where? — Which? — Who? — Why?

1) Question: _____
   _____
   (Key vocabulary: bus / go / airport)
   Answer: Yes, the bus goes at the airport.

2) Question: _____
   _____
   (Key vocabulary: bus / leave)
   Answer: It leaves in ten minutes.

3) Question: _____
   _____
   (Key vocabulary: time)
   Answer: It's half past eight.

4) Question: _____
   _____
   (Key vocabulary: bus / leave from)
   Answer: It goes from the stop over there.

5) *Question:* _____
_____

(Key vocabulary: stop / you / mean)
Answer: Stop 6, just by the cafe.

6) *Question:* _____
_____

(Key vocabulary: ticket / cost)
Answer: A ticket costs £6.50.

7) *Question:* _____
_____

(Key vocabulary: passengers / bus / carry)
Answer: The bus has seats for 36 passengers.

8) *Question:* _____
_____

(Key vocabulary: check / ticket)
Answer: The driver will check your ticket.

9) *Question:* _____
_____

(Key vocabulary: you / go / airport / too)
Answer: Yes, I am.

10) *Question:* _____
_____

(Key vocabulary: you / go / airport)
Answer: Because I am going on my holidays.

Their, There:
Choosing the Correct Forms of Words

Quiz 90

There are a great many hurdles over which the average English-speaker may trip. In this quiz, you need to complete the sentences by choosing the correct word from the list of commonly confused words below. Use each word only once.

it's — its — fewer — less — there — their — they're — that — which — whom — who's — whose

1) _____ the way of the world.
2) I have _____ hours free in the week now than I did when I was working full-time.
3) _____ was an old woman who lived in a shoe.
4) I don't understand _____ reasons for leaving.
5) I need to spend _____ money on taxis.
6) I don't know _____ responsible for keeping the park tidy.
7) That is Steve, _____ you met at the party at New Year.
8) The house, _____ was at the end of the street, suited him perfectly.
9) _____ the most promising students in the whole year.
10) It was the lack of privacy _____ drove him to find a new place to live.
11) I could not see _____ point.
12) 'I like to know _____ breakfast I'm eating,' said Goldilocks.

Sounds Similar: Commonly Confused Words

As if the English language was not tricky enough, we have to contend with a long list of words that sound the same but have different spellings and often entirely unrelated meanings. ~~They're Their~~ There are no hard and fast rules to guide you on this issue but you will get more comfortable distinguishing between them with experience.

Quiz 91

Here are a few commonly mixed-up pairs of words. Can you work out which one should go in which gap?

1) My driving instructor told me to _____ my night driving by picking up Little Johnny from his football _____.
   o Practice/Practise

2) 'Mobile phones are not _____ in class,' said the teacher _____ so that all the students could hear her.
   o Aloud/Allowed

3) When Fred noticed the hole in his _____, the colour drained from his face and he went quite _____.
   o Pale/Pail

4) The view from our _____ was exquisite as we flew low over the _____.
   o Plane/Plain

Answers on page 216

5) Having _____ words that sound the same but that are spelled differently is just _____ confusing!
    o Two/Too

6) Our car was at this end of the car park but _____ car was over _____.
    o Their/There

7) She tried to walk _____ the shoe shop but when she saw those Manolo Blahnik's in the window, she knew she had to _____ them.
    o Buy/By

8) 'We _____ all forms of payment _____ credit cards,' said the shop's owner
    o Accept/Except

9) My favourite watch has a strap that is too _____ for me. I am afraid that I will _____ it.
    o Loose/Lose

10) As our train stood _____ on the track, I penned a letter of complaint to the rail operator on my personalized _____.
    o Stationary/Stationery

11) He knew the grammar quiz book might _____ him emotionally but was surprised its _____ lasted so long.
    o Affect/Effect

How Are You Spelling That? (Part 1)

Quiz 92

English is full of words that seem designed to be misspelt. Here are twenty testers to tease you. Three spellings each, but which is the correct one?

1)	accross	across	acrross
2)	acommodate	accomodate	accommodate
3)	apparantly	apparently	aparently
4)	basiclly	basicly	basically
5)	bizness	buisness	business
6)	committee	commitee	comittee
7)	definately	definitely	definitley
8)	dissapear	disappear	dissappear
9)	fluorescent	florescent	florescant
10)	foreseeable	forseeable	forseable
11)	harrassment	harassment	harrasment
12)	immediatly	immediately	imediately
13)	liasion	liason	liaison
14)	necessary	neccessary	neccesary
15)	ocurrance	ocurance	occurrence
16)	prefered	preferred	preffered
17)	remember	remeber	remmember
18)	successful	succesful	sucessful
19)	tattoo	tatoo	tatto
20)	unforetunately	unfortunatly	unfortunately

Answers on page 217

A Word or Two: Words That Can Be Written as Either One Word or Two

Certain words are routinely rendered incorrectly. Amongst the most prominent of these are *a lot* and *no one* (very often incorrectly written as *alot* and *no-one*). However, on other occasions it is less clear whether we are dealing with one word or two.

Quiz 93

In the following sentences, work out which form of words is needed to fill the gaps.

1) She got the questions in the test _____.
   (all right / alright)

2) He emerged from the crash unscathed and seemed completely

   _____.

   (all right / alright)

3) Do you know if this chair is taken by _____?
   (any one / anyone)

4) It could belong to _____ of that crowd over there?
   (any one / anyone)

5) Having pooled our money, we had £80 _____.
   (all together / altogether)

6) The United fans were in one pub while the City fans drank

   _____ in another pub.

   (all together / altogether)

7) I _____ get lost in Rome.
(all ways / always)

8) _____ lead to Rome.
(all ways / always)

9) Her _____ life was lacking in excitement.
(every day / everyday)

10) _____ I try to help someone.
(every day / everyday)

11) He had catalogued _____ of his CDs alphabetically.
(every one / everyone)

12) _____ has an opinion.
(every one / everyone)

13) I was too scared to go _____ see the reptiles.
(in to / into)

14) The robbers broke _____ the bank.
(in to / into)

15) _____ someday I'll meet my one true love.
(may be / maybe)

16) Though it _____ that such a wonderful day will never arrive.
(may be / maybe)

17) The man was tried for murder even though _____ was ever found.
(no body / nobody)

Answers on pages 217–18

18) There was _____ there to answer the phone.
(no body / nobody)

19) _____ I feel like starting a new life abroad.
(some times / sometimes)

20) The feeling hits me at _____ more than others.
(some times / sometimes)

I'll Keep This Brief:
Abbreviations

The English language owes much to its Latinate heritage and this is no more evident than in our use of abbreviations based on Latin vocabulary.

Quiz 94

Here are twenty of the most common abbreviations you are likely to encounter. In column A, you will find the abbreviation (with the Latin word or phrase from which it is derived in brackets). Can you match each with the correct English definition from column B?

Answers on page 218

Column A	Column B
1) A.D. (anno domini)	a) Which was to be demonstrated
2) a.m. (ante meridiem)	b) After midday
3) c. (circa)	c) For example
4) cf. (confer)	d) For each year
5) CV (curriculum vitae)	e) In the year of the Lord
6) et al. (et alii)	f) After what has been written
7) etc. (et cetera)	g) May he/she rest in peace
8) e.g. (exempli gratia)	h) Teacher of philosophy
9) ibid. (ibidem)	i) Method of operating
10) i.e. (id est)	j) Before midday
11) M.A. (magister artium)	k) Course of life / account of one's life
12) M.O. (modus operandi)	l) Namely / that is to say
13) N.B. (nota bene)	m) Around / about / approximately
14) p.a. (per annum)	n) And the others / and other things
15) Ph.D. (philosophiæ doctor)	o) And others...
16) p.m. (post meridiem)	p) I n the same book / passage / article
17) P.S. (post scriptum)	q) Note well
18) Q.E.D. (quod erat demonstrandum)	r) That is / in other words
19) R.I.P. (requiescat in pace)	s) Bring together / compare
20) viz. (videlicet)	t) Master of arts

Answers on page 218

Your Number's Up!: Roman Numerals

The Romans did much for us, including giving us a number system until it was replaced by the Arabic version we use to this day. Now, you probably only see Roman numerals on clocks, the odd engraving or at the end of the credits on TV, but it's worth having an idea of how the system works. So can you say what number each of the following numerals represents?

Quiz 95

1) X
2) C
3) D
4) I
5) L
6) V
7) M

Before We Start: Prefixes

A prefix is a group of letters placed at the beginning of a word to modify its meaning.

Quiz 96

Here are some common prefixes along with some basic definitions. Can you match each prefix to its correct definition?

Prefix	Meaning
1) a- / an- / in- / un- / non-	a) under at a lower position
2) ab-	b) more than, more than normal
3) ad-	c) across
4) anti- / counter-	d) not
5) dis-	e) between, among
6) extra-	f) inside, within
7) hemi- / semi-	g) excessively, completely
8) hyper-	h) again
9) inter-	i) favouring, in support of
10) intra-	j) away, from
11) over-	k) indicating negation, removal, expulsion
12) post-	l) half
13) pre- / ante-	m) changing into, moving towards, increasing
14) pro-	n) before, preceding
15) re-	o) beyond
16) sub-	p) after in time or order
17) trans-	q) opposing, against, the opposite
18) ultra-	r) outside

Quiz 97

Complete the following sentences by adding appropriate prefixes to the words in bold type, so ensuring that the sentences make better sense.

1) He did not believe in God. He was a self-proclaimed _____**theist**.

2) Just as the opposition were attacking, Manchester United scored on the _____**-attack**.

3) The soldiers shot down the plane using their _____**-aircraft** gun.

4) Having spent much less on his campaign, the electoral candidate was at a serious _____**advantage**.

5) The little boy passed wind during the church service even though he knew it was _____**appropriate**.

6) I wanted to stay sober so I had the _____**-alcoholic** beer.

7) Having completed his journey he _____**mounted** from his bicycle.

8) She considered his behaviour at the party, when he had made a pass at her mother, completely _____ **acceptable**.

All's Well That Ends Well: Suffixes

Suffixes are letters or groups of letters placed at the end of a word to turn it into a new word. There are two principal types of suffix to consider. Firstly, we have *inflectional suffixes*, which do not actually change the meaning of a word but might, for instance, conjugate a verb or make a noun plural.

So *–s* is a suffix used to create plurals, while *–ed* is a suffix that can denote the past tense. We've been covering this type elsewhere in the book, so let's turn our attention to the other sort: *derivational suffixes*.

Derivational suffixes do change the meaning of a word, though the meaning remains related to that of the stem word. More to the point, they can change one type of word into another. Magic! So, for instance, the addition of a simple *–ly* can change an adjective into an adverb (e.g. *hopeful* to *hopefully*). Similarly, suffixes like *–ize* and *–ate* can change nouns into verbs (e.g. *demon* to *demonize* and *hyphen* to *hyphenate*).

Bear in mind a few rules about how suffixes affect spelling. If a word ends in a consonant followed by a *y*, the *y* changes to an *i*. If the word ends in an *e*, the *e* is generally knocked off.

Quiz 98

In this quiz, use each of the available suffixes only once to turn the words listed into different, though related, nouns.

-al — -tion — -cian — -er — -ment — -ness — -sion — -y

Old word	New noun
1) investigate	
2) divide	
3) bank	
4) victor	
5) statistic	
6) empty	
7) place	
8) arrive	

Quiz 99

Use each of the available suffixes only once to turn the nouns listed into related adjectives.

-able — -al — -ary — -ful — -ly — -y —

Noun	Adjective
1) lace	
2) sister	
3) pity	
4) incident	
5) reaction	
6) quote	

Answers on page 220

Trying to Place You: Demonyms

Quiz 100

Demonym is the technical word for the name given to the resident of a specific locality. So, for instance, a resident of Berlin has the demonym, *Berliner*. But not all demonyms are so straightforward. Below are the names of fifteen major cities. What would you call their inhabitants?

1) Sydney	
2) Naples	
3) Munich	
4) Moscow	
5) Mexico City	
6) Liverpool	
7) Las Vegas	
8) Ho Chi Minh City	
9) Guadalajara	
10) Glasgow	
11) Florence	
12) Caracas	
13) Cape Town	
14) Cambridge	
15) Bologna	

Repeat After Me: Tautology

Quiz 101

In a tautological phrase, the speaker or writer uses two or more words with the same meaning unnecessarily. This can lead to them being called a 'stupid idiot', though of course, 'stupid idiot' is itself tautological (for what other sort of idiot is there than a stupid one?). Can you spot the tautological phrases in the exercise below?

1) She couldn't choose which paint to have so they showed her a variety of different colours
2) It is a true fact that Charles Dickens wrote *Oliver Twist*.
3) Tony went to Wembley Stadium to see U2. That his second favourite band, Coldplay, was also on the bill was a real added bonus.
4) I was worn out after I climbed up the mountain.
5) My wife and I get on brilliantly even though we are complete opposites.
6) He is the only person in the world who can play the piano whilst suspended from a crane and wearing a straitjacket. His talents are very unique.
7) The defendant stood in the dock and told the judge that his testimony was the honest truth.
8) Daphne brought a magazine for herself every week, her choice usually based on which title was offering the best free gift.
9) When the old man was caught leaving the shop without paying for his shopping, he was adamant that it was an accidental mistake.
10) Though Charles the Consultant suggested a thousand different solutions to the problem, the end result was always the same.

Answers on page 221

How Are You Spelling That? (Part 2)

Quiz 102

Here are some more testing spellings. Choose the correct spelling from the three options.

1) achieve	acheive	acheve
2) aggressive	agressive	aggresive
3) asassination	assasination	assassination
4) bizarre	bizzare	bizzarre
5) collegue	colleague	coleague
6) conscious	concious	concsious
7) dilema	dilemna	dilemma
8) embarras	embarass	embarrass
9) foregn	foriegn	foreign
10) government	goverment	governmant
11) humorous	humourous	humouros
12) independant	independent	indipendent
13) millenium	millennium	milenium
14) occasion	ocassion	occassion
15) possesion	posession	possession
16) recieve	receive	receve
17) seperate	separate	seperete
18) superseed	supercede	supersede
19) tomorrow	tommorow	tommorrow
20) whereever	wherever	werever

Is Their Alot Wrong With This Centence?: The Ultimate Tester

Quiz 103

To finish, the ultimate test of your English grammar know-how: fourteen sentences, each featuring a grammatical error. But can you spot them?

1) Between you and I, this sentence seems perfectly fine to me.
2) If I was you, I would do all I could to take full marks in the exam.
3) An average of 50,000 people attend games at the new stadium.
4) Less than fifteen people have stepped on the Moon.
5) Due to the absence of rain, all the plants in my garden perished.
6) Nancy Mitford was the older of the six Mitford sisters.
7) The defendant's explanation for his presence at the crime scene did not bear close scrutiny.
8) Its none of my concern whose been given the job instead of me.
9) I question if there is enough grammar education in schools?
10) Running across the beach, a large, jagged shell cut Pamela's foot.
11) I think therefore I am.
12) The patient had an infection and needed antibiotics, so the doctor proscribed some for her.
13) He looked very fine in his new dress shirt and jacket.
14) It was not my intention to end the book on a low note, so I hope this is not too enraging a quiz to have left you with.

Answers on pages 222–4

THE ANSWERS

Answers to Quiz 1

1)	noun	a 'naming' word for a person, thing or place	house, man, New York
2)	verb	a 'doing' word that describes an action or a state of being	to have, to run, to eat
3)	pronoun	a word used as a substitute for a noun, usually referring to a participant in the sentence or a noun already mentioned	I, him, something
4)	adjective	a word that describes a noun	green, funny, sad
5)	adverb	a word that adds meaning to a verb	eagerly, fast, freely
6)	preposition	a word used before a noun or pronoun to express the relationship between it and another object	at, in, near
7)	conjunction	a 'joining' word that links together sentences, phrases or clauses	and, but, until
8)	interjection	a 'stand-alone' word that expresses emotion	boo, hurray, ouch

Answers to Quiz 2

a) *Nouns*

1) day

2) dad / book

3) dog / vet

4) man / park

5) teachers / schools

b) *Verbs*

1) runs

2) see

3) loves / meets

4) have visited

5) will be finishing

c) *Pronouns*

1) I

2) her

3) I / this / I / those

4) He / himself

5) I / yours

d) *Adjectives*

1) twinkling

2) clumsy

3) impressed, helpful

4) boorish

5) golden

e) *Adverbs*

1) angrily

2) angelically

3) drunkenly

4) gaudily

5) melodramatically

f) *Prepositions*

1) near

2) round

3) beyond

4) during

5) through

g) *Conjunctions*

1) and

2) until

3) Either / or

4) in order that

5) as long as

h) *Interjections*

1) Good grief!

2) Goodbye!

3) Yes!

4) Encore!

5) Shh!

Answers to Quiz 3

When (**conjunction**) I (**pronoun**) was (**verb**) a (**adjective**) child (**noun**), I (**pronoun**) loved (**verb**) to (**preposition**) learn (**verb**) new (**adjective**) words (**noun**) but (**conjunction**) only (**adverb**) now (**adverb**) am (**verb**) I (**pronoun**) truly (**adverb**) starting (**verb**) to (**preposition**) understand (**verb**) the (**adjective**) complexities (**noun**) of (**preposition**) the (**adjective**) language (**noun**). Wow (**interjection**), thank (**verb**) goodness (**noun**) that (**conjunction**) I (**pronoun**) have (**verb**) this (**adjective**) book (**noun**) to (**preposition**) help (**verb**) me (**pronoun**)!

Answers to Quiz 4

1) abstract
2) proper
3) concrete
4) proper
5) concrete
6) proper
7) abstract
8) concrete
9) abstract
10) proper

Answers to Quiz 5

armpit
bull's-eye
bicycle seat
cat burglar
chopstick
doorbell
dry-cleaning
fingerprint
girlfriend
lawsuit
lion tamer
mother-in-law

nightclub

painkiller

passer-by

pear tree

penknife

science-fiction

train-spotter

tugboat

Answers to Quiz 6

1) Non-countable
2) Countable
3) Non-countable
4) Non-countable
5) Non-countable
6) Countable
7) Countable
8) Non-countable
9) Countable

Answers to Quiz 7

1) **A lot of** people have problems with grammar.
2) I think I got **the majority of** questions right.
3) I only drink **a little** coffee because caffeine can give me a headache.
4) With the deadline approaching, there was **not much** time left.
5) Though **some** of the city was destroyed, **a great deal** remained standing
6) He woke up with a headache, having drunk **too much** wine last night.
7) He was sick after he ate **half** the cake.
8) His essay was marked down for **a lack of** attention to detail.
9) He had three tickets for the game so he took **a couple of** friends.
10) She catalogued **all** the library's books.

Answers to Quiz 8

1) I have **some** loose change in my pocket.
2) We never go **anywhere**.
3) I don't have **any** idea what to buy her for a gift.
4) They don't know **anybody** in Canada.
5) I know **someone** who will be able to help.
6) Would you like to go **somewhere** for the weekend if I pay for your ticket?
7) 'I don't know **anything**,' the defendant cried out.
8) Is there **any** cheese in the fridge?
9) Could you pour me **some** coffee?
10) She knew **something** that she wasn't telling him.

Answers to Quiz 9

Singular	Plural
1) buffalo	buffaloes
2) chief	chiefs
3) church	churches
4) cliff	cliffs
5) dish	dishes
6) dress	dresses
7) fax	faxes
8) fish	fish or fishes
9) hoof	hoofs or hooves
10) key	keys
11) lady	ladies
12) life	lives
13) proof	proofs
14) scarf	scarfs or scarves
15) solo	solos
16) thief	thieves
17) tomato	tomatoes
18) torch	torches
19) waltz	waltzes
20) zoo	zoos

Answers to Quiz 10

c[1]	a[2]	c	t	i				b[3]		d[4]
	l				p[5]	m[6]	e	d	i	a
q[7]	u	i	z		e		a			t
	m			c[8]	o	d		u		a
	n			p		o[9]	x			
d[10]	i	c	e		l		a			
				g[11]	e	e	s	e		n[12]
f[13]	l[14]	e		e		e		e		
u	i	n		s				b		
n[15]	u	c	l	e	i			b[16]	u	s
g		e	r					l		
i		a[17]	n	t	e	n	n	a	e	

Answers to Quiz 11

1)	+ h)	crew of sailors
2)	+ j)	choir of singers
3)	+ e)	fleet of ships
4)	+ f)	bouquet of flowers
5)	+ i)	flock of sheep
6)	+ b)	gaggle of geese
7)	+ d)	library of books
8)	+ g)	school of fish
9)	+ a)	pack of wolves
10)	+ c)	herd of elephants

Answers to Quiz 12

1)	+ e)	cackle of hyenas
2)	+ h)	charm of finches
3)	+ k)	colony of bats
4)	+ n)	intrusion of cockroaches
5)	+ g)	knot of toads
6)	+ d)	labour of moles
7)	+ c)	murder of crows
8)	+ m)	parliament of owls
9)	+ o)	plague of locusts
10)	+ i)	pod of dolphins
11)	+ b)	pride of lions
12)	+ a)	shrewdness of apes
13)	+ f)	smack of jellyfish
14)	+ j)	streak of tigers
15)	+ l)	unkindness of ravens

Answers to Quiz 13

1) Many of the squadron **were lost** in that battle.
2) The squadron **has lost** all of its men in the attack.
3) The crowd **was singing** as one.
4) The crowd **were fighting** amongst themselves.
5) The entire class **was taking** the exam.
6) The class **were working** on several projects.
7) The staff **were showing** signs of tension.
8) The whole staff **has walked** out on strike.
9) The jury **was sent** away to consider its verdict.
10) The jury **were unable** to agree on a verdict.

Answers to Quiz 14

1) I need to buy **a** new pen.
2) Can you pass me **the** pen next to you.
3) Pete is top scorer in **the** school football team.

183

4) There were no spare seats on the bus as **a** football team had got on at the previous stop.
5) London is **a** wonderful city.
6) London is **the** capital city of England.

Answers to Quiz 15

1) We went to Paris last week for lunch. **The** restaurant was fantastic.
2) It was next door to **the** hotel where we stayed last year.
3) I had **a** glass of wine and **a** bowl of snails.
4) My friend had **the** horse.
5) At first, our waiter brought us baguettes and Brie. It was **an** honest mistake.
6) We took so long eating that we had to rush to get to **the** station.
7) Then we got stuck in **the** Channel Tunnel for **an** hour and **a** half.
8) When we got into London, it was so late that we decided to get **a** taxi home.
9) I was so tired that I told my friend that I needed **a** holiday.
10) 'Perhaps **a** European tour by train,' my friend said.

Answers to Quiz 16

1) I am going to **India** next week.
2) Have you been to **the Eiffel Tower**?
3) Sherlock Holmes had rooms on **Baker Street**.
4) We are going to **the Museum of Modern Art**.
5) It is sometimes said that you can see **the Great Wall of China** from space.
6) The capital of Mongolia is **Ulan Bator**.
7) The couple opened a dry-cleaners on **the High Street**.
8) There are some wonderful cheeses made in **the Netherlands**.
9) We went from Buckingham Palace to **Westminster Abbey**.
10) Laurence Olivier helped found **the National Theatre**.
11) The plane landed at **London Heathrow Airport**.
12) The River Nile is longer than **the Mississippi**.

13) We had fun pretending to prop up **the Leaning Tower of Pisa**.
14) The British sometimes refer to Australia and New Zealand as **the Antipodes**.
15) There are some wonderful distilleries in **the south of Ireland**.
16) We love wine tasting in **southern France**.

Answers to Quiz 17

	Nominative	*Accusative*	*Possessive*
1st person singular	I	me	mine
2nd person singular	you	you	yours
3rd person singular	he, she, it	him, her, it	his, hers, its
1st person plural	we	us	ours
2nd person plural	you	you	yours
3rd person plural	they	them	theirs

Answers to Quiz 18

1) Toby's mother told **him** to do his homework.
2) Toby told **her** that he didn't want to do **it**.
3) The Greek government want the Elgin Marbles returned as they believe them to be **theirs**.
4) Claire went to see her boss, Jack, but **he** wasn't available to see **her**.
5) I wanted to buy my neighbour's car but I couldn't afford **it**.
6) Walter had a toy that he didn't want to share with his sister. 'It's **mine**, it's not **yours**,' he screamed.
7) My wife and I wanted to go on holiday so **we** went to the travel agency.
8) Our house is large so we invited all our friends to spend the weekend at **ours**.

Answers to Quiz 19

1) You have to stop doing this to **yourself**.
2) We treated **ourselves** to dinner at the new restaurant in town.
3) She knew what she wanted for **herself**.

4) When you're away on holiday, be sure to look after **yourselves**.
5) The monkey was scratching **itself** with a stick.
6) Count Dracula could not see **himself** in the mirror.
7) They could not be trusted to behave **themselves**.
8) I kicked **myself** when I heard the correct answer.

Answer to Quiz 20

1) You could tell that Allie and Fred loved **each other** just by being around them.
2) The group of children could not stop teasing **one another**.
3) When they heard that the job had gone to someone else, the five interviewees commiserated with **one another**.
4) After the competition ended in a draw, the two competitors congratulated **each other**.

Answers to Quiz 21

1) Those **whom** are blessed with beauty must avoid vanity.
2) The play **that** I directed was well received by the critics.
3) He juggled three flaming torches as he unicycled around the Big Top, **which** was something no one had ever done before.
4) The boy **whose** feet were webbed was the best swimmer in the county.
5) The cab driver **who** took us to the airport didn't know the way.

Answers to Quiz 22

1) In space, **no one** can hear you scream.
2) Leave the chocolates alone; there are only **a few** left.
3) I am sure I saw **someone** up at the window.
4) Her best friend had dated **several** celebrities.
5) When questioned, the witness denied he had seen **anything**.
6) Have a look in the box. There's **something** for you.
7) What a great party. **Everyone** had a wonderful time!
8) The good news called for champagne, but sadly they didn't have **any**.
9) There were several thousand spectators and **all** had a good time.
10) I need a good lawyer. Do you know **one**?

Answers to Quiz 23

1) What time is it?
2) Which school did you go to?
3) Who designed this building?
4) What is your profession?
5) Whose t-shirt is Kate wearing?
6) Whom did he vote for at the last election?
7) Which car are you going to drive?
8) Who borrowed the spare umbrella?

Answers to Quiz 24

1) I got **this** at the market.
2) Take **those** to the charity shop.
3) I'm taking **these** to the cleaners.
4) Take **that** home with you and study it.

Answers to Quiz 25

1) **These books** are all overdue.
2) Is **this seat** free, please?
3) I live in **that castle** on the hill.
4) Does my bum look big in **this dress**?
5) Are **those glasses** yours?
6) Do you know any of **these people**?
7) Listen to **those birds** singing.
8) How much is **that dog** in the window?

Answers to Quiz 26

1) I don't know **whom** to believe.
2) He admired George Washington, **who** was the first President of the United States of America.
3) Do you know **whose** wallet this is?
4) I'm very grateful to Ken, **who's** going to give me a lift to work.
5) **Who** ate the last biscuit?
6) **Whose** car are you going in?
7) **Who's** going to come with me to the shops?
8) To **whom** should I address my letter?

Answers to Quiz 27

The Answers

1) Biro
2) Sellotape (or Scotch Tape)
3) Frisbee
4) Bloomers
5) Velcro
6) Winnebago
7) Tupperware
8) Leotard
9) MacIntosh
10) Post-it Notes
11) Hoover
12) Jacuzzi

Answers to Quiz 28

Infinitive	past participle	present participle
allow	allowed	allowing
call	called	calling
live	lived	living
cry	cried	crying
study	studied	studying
sin	sinned	sinning
tie	tied	tying
develop	developed	developing
embarrass	embarrassed	embarrassing
meddle	meddled	meddling
race	raced	racing
nod	nodded	nodding

Answers to Quiz 29

	present	*past*
I	am	was
you	are	were
he/she/it	is	was
we	are	were
you	are	were
they	are	were

present participle	being
past participle	been

Answers to Quiz 30

	present	*past*
I	have	had
you	have	had
he/she/it	has	had
we	have	had
you	have	had
they	have	had

present participle	having
past participle	had

Answers to Quiz 31

	present	*past*
I	do	did
you	do	did
he/she/it	does	did
we	do	did
you	do	did
they	do	did

present participle	*doing*
past participle	*done*

Answers to Quiz 32

	present	*past*
I	go	went
you	go	went
he/she/it	goes	went
we	go	went
you	go	went
they	go	went

present participle	*going*
past participle	*gone*

Answers to Quiz 33

arise	arose	arisen
bear	bore	borne
become	became	become
begin	began	begun

bite	bit	bitten
blow	blew	blown
break	broke	broken
bring	brought	brought
burst	burst	burst
buy	bought	bought
choose	chose	chosen
cut	cut	cut
do	did	done
draw	drew	drawn
drive	drove	driven
eat	ate	eaten
fall	fell	fallen
feel	felt	felt
fly	flew	flown
forget	forgot	forgotten
forsake	forsook	forsaken
freeze	froze	frozen
go	went	gone
have	had	had
hide	hid	hidden
know	knew	known
lie	lay	lain
mistake	mistook	mistaken
ride	rode	ridden
ring	rang	rung
see	saw	seen
shake	shook	shaken
sing	sang	sung
speak	spoke	spoken
steal	stole	stolen
swear	swore	sworn
swell	swelled	swollen
tear	tore	torn
throw	threw	thrown
write	wrote	written

Answer to Quiz 34

1)

The subject is **He**.

The object is **car**.

2)

The subject is **she**.

The object is **company**.

3)

The subject is **locksmith**.

The object is **keys**.

4)

The subject is **rugby player**.

The object is **try**.

5)

The subject is **soldier**.

The object is **gun**.

Answers to Quiz 35

1) students
2) her
3) secretary
4) me
5) Anna

Answers to Quiz 36

1) She **sneezed** so hard that she almost fell over.
2) She **wept** pitifully for hours.
3) I **am going** (or I **went**) to Canada.
4) The building **collapsed** after the earthquake.
5) They **stayed** at the best hotel in town.

Answers to Quiz 37

1) Intransitive
2) Transitive
3) Intransitive
4) Intransitive
5) Transitive
6) Transitive
7) Transitive
8) Intransitive
9) Intransitive
10) Transitive

Answers to Quiz 38

1) passive
2) active
3) passive
4) active
5) active
6) passive
7) passive
8) active

Answers to Quiz 39

1) Dinner was served by the waiter.
2) The car was driven by Fred.
3) The penalty was scored by the defender.
4) *Romeo and Juliet* was written by William Shakespeare.
5) The green dress was worn by Laura.
6) My class is taught by Mr Wilson.
7) Those racing pigeons are trained by Uncle Arthur.
8) The birthday cake will be eaten by us tomorrow.
9) That picture was painted by a child.
10) My homework was copied by Tommy.

Answers to Quiz 40

A) Present Simple

I **eat** fish and chips.

He **goes** to the cinema.

They **run** a cafe.

You **walk** to work.

B) Present Continuous

I **am learning** Japanese.

He **is listening** to music.

You **are watching** a movie.

They **are fighting**.

C) Present Perfect

We **have gone** to Lisbon.

You **have seen** the Great Barrier Reef.

I **have written** a novel.

They **have bought** a house.

D) Present Perfect Continuous

I **have been running** round the park.

You **have been missing** lectures.

They **have been surfing** every day.

It **has been broken** for a month.

E) Simple Past

I **walked** into town.

You **chose** some new shoes.

He **lost** his wallet.

We **played** tennis.

F) Past Continuous

You **were driving** your car.

They **were climbing** a mountain.

We **were flying** in a helicopter.

She **was designing** a dress.

194

G) Imperfect

We **used to throw** parties every week.

I **used to paint** watercolours.

You **used to work** in Brussels.

They **used to attend** my school.

H) Past Perfect

I **had paid** the bill at the restaurant.

It **had fallen** off the shelf.

They **had sold** their car.

You **had asked** for a big present.

I) Future

I **shall meet** you at the cinema.

You **will wear** your favourite scarf.

It **will rain** tomorrow.

We **shall win** the lottery this weekend!

J) Future Continuous

I **shall be studying** in Italy next year.

You **will be staying** with your family at Christmas.

We **shall be dining** at the Savoy on Tuesday.

He **shall be running** the country this time next year!

K) Future Perfect Continuous

I **shall have been** at university for five years by the time I graduate.

The clock **will have been** standing in that corner for a hundred years next year.

You **will have been** cooking that chicken for two hours soon!

We **shall have been** married for five years in October.

L) Future Perfect

I **shall have completed** my degree by next summer.

You **will have won** an Oscar by the time you're thirty.

We **shall have lived** in five countries when we move to Australia.

They **will have lifted** the cup five times if they beat their opponents in the big match.

195

Answers to Quiz 41

1) Dave **is reading** *The Great Gatsby* by F. Scott Fitzgerald at school this term.
2) He **has been reading** his novel for the last week.
3) She **enjoys** reading every night before bed.
4) She **has loved** reading all her life.

Answers to Quiz 42:
A Postcard from New York,

Dear Pam and Bob,

Well, we **are having** the most wonderful time in New York. Our hotel **is** wonderful and the staff **run** around after us. They **have been telling** us about all the best places to visit. We **have eaten** in some wonderful restaurants. Stan **is tucking** into a huge hamburger as I **write** this note!

Today we **are touring** round the city on a bus. We **have visited** Central Park and the Museum of Modern Art. I **have been reading** the guidebook you lent us so **I lecture** Stan about all the places we **are seeing**.

My, how I **love** this city. We **wish** that you were here and **are looking forward** to seeing you very soon.

Missing you both,
Beryl and Stan xx

Answers to Quiz 43

1) Janet **ran** the London Marathon last May.
2) Janet **was running** the marathon for the third year in a row.
3) Janet **used to shudder** at the thought of running such a distance.
4) Janet **had hoped** to beat her record but missed it by ten seconds.

Answers to Quiz 44

THE ROME BUGLE
Ides of March, 182 AD
From our special correspondent at the Empire Games

Yesterday **was** the opening day of the Games at the Colosseum and an expectant crowd **greeted** the Emperor Commodus ecstatically. The crowd **was entertained** by a packed programme of contests and when the spectators left, they **were wanting** more.

Early in the morning the heavens **had opened** so spectators **took** shelter beneath the stadium's vast awning. 'It **was raining** for at least three hours,' one crowd-member told me. 'But we **have enjoyed** ourselves still. My own father **used to say** how the Games always **used to bring** the rain!'

As has become the custom, in the first bout after lunch, brave Commodus himself **fought** a prisoner-of-war who **had been chosen** especially for the honour. The two men **were locked** in fierce combat for many minutes before the Emperor at last **triumphed**. The prisoner **was not killed** as a gesture of the Emperor's mercy.

It is said that the Emperor **had wrestled** a fierce tiger in preparation for the match. He was quoted as saying, 'When I was a boy, I **used to watch** the gladiators and **dreamed** of being one. I have worked hard all my life to stay fit and strong. These last six weeks I **was training** especially hard for my match today. I **walked** into the arena this afternoon full of confidence and I **left** it the victor.'

Answers to Quiz 45

1) Max **will be taking** his driving test next month.
2) He **will arrive** at the examination centre at 9 a.m. on Friday the 4th.
3) He **will have been learning** to drive for six months.
4) He **will have had** 24 lessons by the time of the test.

Answers to Quiz 46

1) You **shall** do as you're told.
2) Cinderella **will** go to the ball.
3) They promised they **shall** reimburse me fully.
4) I **shall** pick you up in the morning.
5) They **will** go for a ride on the London Eye during their holiday.
6) **Will** I pass my exams?
7) **Shall** I get your coat for you?

Answers to Quiz 47

NASA PRESS RELEASE
20 September 2025

Tomorrow NASA **will launch** its first manned vessel to Mars. The team of three astronauts **will be travelling** for several months and, after docking, **will stay** on the planet for five days. By the time they land, each astronaut **will have eaten** 500 dehydrated meals and **will have lost** up to a stone in weight.

The mission leader, Capt. Dwight Starblaze, **will be carrying** out a series of experiments to discover if there is life on the Red Planet. He **will be leaving** a time capsule full of artefacts from Earth for alien life-forms to discover. By the end of the trip, Capt. Starblaze **will have completed** his forty-second trip outside of the Earth's atmosphere.

Capt. Starblaze told journalists: 'By the end of this mission, I **shall have been working** on space missions for over twenty years. I have told my wife that, once I'm back on Earth, I **shall retire** as I **shall have fulfilled** all my childhood dreams. I must pay credit too to the members of my team, who **will continue** the good work of NASA: Stella Burst, who herself **will have been searching** for Martian life for ten years by the time we return; and Kirk Moondust, who **will return** to complete a PhD in Martianology next year.'

Answers to Quiz 48

1) The doctor **will** see you tomorrow.
2) I **couldn't** believe my eyes.
3) The dog **had been** waiting an hour for his walk.
4) I **have** eaten too much.
5) He **ought to** take his driving test soon.
6) We **should have been** going on holiday today but it **was** cancelled.
7) You **do** paint beautifully.
8) They **must have** caught the last bus home.
9) I **might** try to buy a new house.
10) I **am** going to the cinema.
11) Who **would have** thought it was possible?
12) I **can't be** blamed for that.

Answers to Quiz 49

1) Imperative.
2) Subjunctive.
3) Indicative.
4) Imperative.
5) Indicative.
6) Indicative.
7) Subjunctive.

Answers to Quiz 50

1) May the force **be** with you!
2) He proposed that she **buy** his half of the business.
3) If we **were to run** our own restaurant, who would look after the kids? (run)
4) If I **were to take** that job, I would have to work long hours.
5) She wished that she **were** slimmer so she could buy those new jeans.
6) She suggests she **book** a table for next Saturday.
7) Would you take the job if you **were** me?

Answers to Quiz 51

1) Third conditional
2) Zero conditional
3) First conditional
4) First conditional
5) Third conditional
6) Second conditional
7) Zero conditional
8) Second conditional

Answers to Quiz 52

1) It is dangerous **not** to drive slowly.
2) I **do not** want to be unpopular.
3) I am **not** as rich as King Midas.
4) My time machine is **not** working.
5) With the headmaster's words ringing in her ears, she set off down the corridor, **not** running.
6) I am too cautious **not** to pay my insurance premium.
7) I have **not** met them before.
8) I **do not** have a fleet of private aeroplanes.
9) He **did not** propose to her on a hill overlooking Florence.
10) I **do not** do my French homework each weekend.

Answers to Quiz 53

1) I didn't do anything!
2) There is nowhere I'd rather be than here with you.
3) I have not been late for college all term.
4) There's not anything I don't know.
5) I haven't been out anywhere all night.
6) There's not anyone who will do the job better than me.

Answers to Quiz 54

1) a) Must we not go?
   b) Mustn't we go?
2) a) Would you not like to try the wine?
   b) Wouldn't you like to try the wine
3) a) Have you not seen enough?
   b) Haven't you seen enough?
4) a) Should they not go there?
   b) Shouldn't they go there.
5) a) Is it not warm outside?
   b) Isn't it warm outside?

Answers to Quiz 55

1) Wonderfully **directed** by Luc Besson, the film was a triumph.
2) **Invested** wisely, your money can give you a good return.
3) **Opening** his door, he was hit with a snowball.
4) **Being** new to the company, he was keen to make a good impression.
5) The drink got him in the end, **destroying** his liver.
6) The ancient city was lost to history, **covered** by tons of sand.
7) The lecturer droned on, **boring** the students.
8) **Saddened** by the news, she shed a tear.
9) The signs were covered up, **confusing** the tourists.
10) **Surprised** by the size of the present, he almost fell off his chair.
11) **Smelling** the roses, the gardener thought how much he loved his job.
12) They opened the bottle of wine **brought** by their friends from France.
13) There was nothing left of the photograph, **burnt** in the flames.
14) They listened to the announcements, **spoken** by the station manager.

Answers to Quiz 56

1) participle
2) gerund
3) gerund
4) participle
5) gerund
6) participle
7) gerund
8) gerund
9) participle
10) gerund
11) participle
12) gerund

Answers to Quiz 57

.	full stop	denotes the end of a standard sentence.
?	question mark	denotes a direct question.
!	exclamation mark	an alternative to the full stop used to grab the reader's attention or to indicate strong emotion.
—	dash	used either alone or as one of a pair (in place of parenthesis) to introduce an aside, an interruption or a new piece of information, to indicate a sudden change in emotion or thought, or to show the omission of words.
-	hyphen	used either to break a long word at the end of a line of text or to link two words together.
"	quotation mark	denotes direct speech.
:	colon	denotes that the following text summarizes or explains the preceding part of the sentence.
;	semicolon	used to join two or more independent clauses that don't really deserve to be sentences in themselves.

	comma	denotes a pause or a separate clause within a sentence.
'	apostrophe	denotes either possession or the contraction of two words (when it is used in place of the omitted letter or letters).

Answers to Quiz 58

1) Fire! Run for your lives!
2) It was so cold that I had to wear my hat, gloves and scarf.
3) 'Give me data,' demanded Sherlock Holmes.
4) Do you know the way to Amarillo?
5) You can't make a silk purse out of a sow's ear.
6) It came to him suddenly in the bath – Eureka!
7) Moscow is the capital city of Russia.
8) She had to pay a large fine on her long-overdue library book.
9) It was the best of times; it was the worst of times.
10) He liked his new job title: Head of Client Relations.

Answers to Quiz 59

Have you read much James Joyce? I enjoyed *Dubliners* particularly. You could understand what he was talking about because he employed commas, full stops, question marks and even apostrophes. That's not the case in *Finnegans Wake*, which was a book I couldn't get on with. My friend loves *Ulysses* most. He told me once, 'It's the best book I have ever read!'

Answers to Quiz 60

a) Incorrect. When 'its' is being used to indicate the possessive, it does not take the apostrophe.
b) Incorrect. The apostrophe in 'shouldn't' is right but there should also be one in 'its', because here it is a contraction of 'it is'.
c) Correct.
d) Incorrect. In the case of two or more individuals jointly possessing an object, an 's' is needed after the last name only. So here we refer to 'Tom and Claire's new house'.

e) Incorrect. The first use of 'banana' should have an apostrophe but the second instance should not.
f) Correct.
g) Incorrect. There is no need to have an apostrophe in 'pizzas'.
h) Correct. This is a really tricky one. Where words end in an –iz or –eeze sound (such as Sophocles), we don't add the final 's' to avoid the word becoming too much of a mouthful.

Answers to Quiz 61

Great Deals at Sid and Joe's Fruit and Veg Shop!

It's price-slashing madness so don't miss out!
Oranges – 50 pence for three.
Fresh pineapple juice – fall in love with its taste!
Spanish tomatoes – your favourite and mine!
Jersey Royal potatoes – they're perfect for the summer!
Yummy strawberry puddings – ideal for children's parties!

Are these the High Street's best deals? Too right! (Much cheaper than John's Farm Foods!)
Only two children at a time and no dogs!
(For more special deals, visit our stall at St Barnabus' Market this Saturday too. You shan't regret it.)

Answers to Quiz 62

1) After going out for a night on the town, I was very sick.
2) His brother attended Keble College, Oxford.
3) I walked through the haunted house, trembling, and was almost in tears by the time I found the exit.
4) We've got an early start tomorrow, so let's get some sleep.
5) Give it a rest, will you?
6) Millie the Dog won first prize in her class and was best in show, too.
7) Yours sincerely, Frank Hobbs
8) The hotel was crumbling, the staff rude.

9) In 1666, the Great Fire of London broke out in Pudding Lane.

10) His favourite bands of all time were The Beatles, The Rolling Stones, The Who and The Spice Girls.

11) In 1940, with Hitler rampaging through Europe, Winston Churchill became Prime Minister.

12) When I was ten years old, in 1986, Diego Maradona led Argentina to the World Cup.

13) Barak Obama, the President of the United States of America, was born in Hawaii.

14) Bagpuss was an old, fat, furry catpuss.

15) The judge asked, 'How do you plead?'

16) There are approximately 60,000,000 living people in the UK.

Answers to Quiz 63

1) 'Give me that!' she demanded rudely.

2) 'I do like it here,' he said quietly.

3) He told me that he was fed up with his grammar homework. (NB There is no need for quotation marks in reported speech.)

4) He said, 'I want to climb Mount Everest.'

5) She said she was sorry for the trouble she'd caused.

6) 'Don't cry,' she said. 'You'll soon feel better.'

7) He reported, 'I heard her whisper "don't leave now" in his ear.'

Answers to Quiz 64

1) We live in a fifth-floor flat.

2) We live on the fifth floor.

3) I felt let down by the producers,

4) After all the excitement beforehand, the show was a complete let-down.

5) She noticed a thick layer of dust round the clock.

6) The politician was not a fan of round-the-clock news.

7) I enjoyed a glass of 20-year-old Scotch.

8) The Scotch is 20 years old,

9) He bowls with his left hand.

10) He was the best left-handed cricketer I ever saw.

11) He was caught in a twelve-mile traffic jam.

12) The traffic jam stretched back for twelve miles.

13) We are going away for two weeks.

14) We are going on a two-week holiday.

Answers to Quiz 65

1) Coco was a **jolly** clown.

2) Her dress was very **elegant**.

3) She enjoyed the occasional glass of **sparkling** wine.

4) The sea was the most inviting **blue**.

5) The motorcyclist was going to jump across the **vast** canyon.

6) The **lazy** dog slept all day.

7) His favourite breakfast was a **greasy** fry-up.

8) The father-of-the-bride was very **proud**.

9) He struggled to get the square peg into a **round** hole.

10) The landing at the airport was very **bumpy**.

11) The headmaster addressed the pupils in a **thundering** voice.

12) The 6' model refused to date **short** men.

13) The athlete tucked into a **nutritious** bowl of salad.

14) The little boy loved his **wooden** train set.

15) The film star had **numerous** gentlemen friends.

Answers to Quiz 66

1) Dickensian

2) Lutheran

3) Kafkaesque

4) Wagnerian

5) Elizabethan

6) Latino

7) Quixotic

8) Titanic

Answers to Quiz 67

1) It **rained heavily**, which was good for the garden.

2) The cat **silently crept** up on the mouse.

3) The children **played** together **nicely**.

4) The policeman **accused** the innocent man **wrongly**.

5) The old man **laughed heartily** at the rude joke.
6) The woman **waited patiently** for the doctor.
7) The audience **applauded enthusiastically** after the great show.
8) The cup-winning team **paraded victoriously**.
9) The dog **slept peacefully** in his bed.
10) The sprinter **ran fast** in the Olympic final.
11) The explorer **approached** the lion **bravely**.
12) The boy **gave** the teacher his homework **nervously**, fearing he had got it all wrong.
13) The teenager **stared** at the beautiful girl next door **longingly**.
14) The lawyer **addressed** the jury **truthfully**.
15) The man **spoke** to the waiter **rudely**.

Answers to Quiz 68

1a) adjective
1b) adverb
2a) adverb
2b) adjective
3a) adjective
3b) adverb
4a) adjective
4b) adverb
5a) adjective
5b) adverb
6a) adverb
6b) adjective

Answers to Quiz 69

1) The lecturer was smart but his colleague was **cleverer**.
2) Uncle Fred weighs a lot but Aunt Edna is **fatter**.
3) The little boy was loud but his sister was **noisier**.
4) Baked beans don't cost much but caviar is **less cheap**.
5) Australia is a long way away but New Zealand is **farther**.
6) Having a cold is bad but having 'flu is **worse**.
7) Alan Sugar has a lot of money but Lakshmi Mittal has **more**.

8) Carl Lewis was speedy but Usain Bolt runs **faster**.
9) The kitten looks sweet but the puppy is **cuter**.
10) Stilton is stinky but your socks are **smellier**.

Answers to Quiz 70

1) Mount Everest is the **tallest** mountain in the world.
2) Platinum is the **most valuable** metal.
3) Lionel Messi is the **best** footballer in the world.
4) The Vatican City is the **smallest** country in the world.
5) The Mona Lisa is the **most famous** painting in the world.
6) Neptune is the **farthest** planet from the Sun.
7) The Nile is the **longest** river in the world.
8) Tokyo is the **most populous** city in the world.
9) Milton was the **most prolific** poet of his age.
10) Jack the Ripper was the **most feared** criminal of the Victorian age.

Answers to Quiz 71

1) He was having dinner with a **beautiful, young** woman.
2) She was particularly interested in acquiring the masterworks of **old, French** watercolourists.
3) She specifically requested that he buy the **Jersey pouring** cream.
4) There were a dozen **large, blue, glass** bottles sitting behind the bar.
5) He was delighted with the **stylish, size-10, golden, running** shoes he'd bought.
6) She always carried around a **big, old, puce, hessian, knitting** bag.
7) The child was fascinated by an **impressive, 19th-century, green, wooden, Swiss-made** cuckoo clock.
8) They lay on a bed covered in the **finest, large, brand new, square, white, cotton, valance** sheet available.

Answers to Quiz 72

1) Bill was **dangerously** ill for a week after the operation.
2) Africa is a **much** bigger continent than Europe.
3) John was **seriously** hurt when he crashed his car.
4) That was **easily** the best first date Kate had ever been on.
5) Deep sea diving on your own is **extremely** dangerous.
6) Sandra is a **highly** accomplished pianist.
7) Winning the lottery was an **absolutely** amazing feeling.
8) I was **really** upset when I heard the bad news.
9) Jan is an **exceptionally** gifted opera singer.
10) A Siberian winter is **bitterly** cold.

Answers to Quiz 73

1) The tigers defended **their** territory ferociously.
2) **Our** neighbours invited us round for a barbecue.
3) It's **my** party and I'll cry if I want to!
4) He was very proud of **his** efforts.
5) Emily enjoyed the way everyone admired **her** new hat.
6) **Your** new job is just perfect for you!
7) The cat leapt in the air when it saw **its** own reflection.

Answers to Quiz 74

1) Simile
2) Metaphor
3) Simile
4) Simile
5) Metaphor

Answers to Quiz 75

1)	+ g)	The killer had a heart of stone.
2)	+ j)	It was raining cats and dogs.
3)	+ h)	His legs had turned to jelly
4)	+ a)	The Moon was a silver dollar suspended in the sky.
5)	+ c)	He is so reliable, he is my rock.
6)	+ i)	I was shocked she married a snake like him.
7)	+ d)	At the dinner table, he's a pig.
8)	+ e)	I looked at myself staring back from the lake that was a mirror glass.
9)	+ f)	He followed her round unthinkingly; he was a sheep.
10)	+ b)	He knows so much; he is a veritable encyclopaedia.

Answers to Quiz 76

1)	+ c)	'Holmes looked at him thoughtfully like a master chess-player who meditates his crowning move.'
2)	+ h)	'O my love is like a red, red rose'.
3)	+ f)	'Her hair was rich as a wild bee's nest and her eyes were full of stings.'
4)	+ b)	'Why, man, he doth bestride the narrow world like a Colossus.'
5)	+ g)	'The very mist on the Essex marshes was like a gauzy and radiant fabric.'
6)	+ e)	'The very mystery of him excited her curiosity like a door that had neither lock nor key.'
7)	+ j)	'Elderly American ladies leaning on their canes listed toward me like towers of Pisa.'
8)	+ a)	'The late afternoon sky bloomed in the window for a moment like the blue honey of the Mediterranean.'
9)	+ d)	'The other was fair, as fair as can be, with great masses of golden hair and eyes like pale sapphires.'
10)	+ i)	'It was not really a happy question to ask him; it was like an examination paper that asks grammar, when what you want to be asked is Kings of England.'

Answers to Quiz 77

1) He had got an A in his A-level maths **even though** he was only ten years old.
2) The teacher looked fierce **but** she was really very kind.
3) He got sent to prison **because** he robbed an old lady.
4) She was rich and famous **yet** still she wasn't happy.
5) She was very tall **and** slim.
6) He went to Paris **so that** he could visit the Eiffel Tower.
7) She left the night club **before** the bouncers threw her out.
8) He wanted to be sure the picture was genuine **if** he was going to pay so much for it.
9) She would go to the concert **provided that** she could get a lift.
10) He will stop taking the medicine **as soon as** he feels better.
11) Heels repaired **while** you wait.
12) She has not worked as hard **since** she came back from her holiday.

Answers to Quiz 78

1)	+ b)	**Both** Terry **and** Chris applied for the same job.
2)	+ c)	**Either** Charlie **or** Bill will give you a lift to the show.
3)	+ a)	**Neither** Russia **nor** the Netherlands have ever won the soccer world cup.
4)	+ e)	I am going on holiday **whether** you go **or** not.
5)	+ d)	He **not only** drove the car **but also** built it from scratch.

Answers to Quiz 79

1) Dave's off to the pub tonight. Dave has not drunk alcohol **since** 20 May.
2) He will be at the gym **from** 7pm **until** 9pm tomorrow.
3) He has tickets for a film **at** 8pm **on** Wednesday evening.
4) He must remember to turn his phone off **during** the movie.
5) Dave doesn't have a free evening **until** Thursday.
6) He will meet Jack **on** Friday **before** going to meet Gerald.
7) He is going to Kelly's party **after** football.

8) Dave must give his front door keys to his neighbour **before** he goes on holiday. The neighbour has agreed to water Dave's plants **until** he gets back.

Answers to Quiz 80

1) Jessica the Cat was sitting **by** the window.
2) She spied a bird flying **in** the sky.
3) The bird landed **on** the lawn.
4) Jessica walked **to** the door and crawled **through** the cat flap.
5) She slunk **under** a bush.
6) She leapt **over** a wall.
7) She crept silently until she was just **behind** the bird.
8) A moment later there was a bird **inside** Jessica's belly and a cat with a big grin **upon** her face.

Answers to Quiz 81

1) Global warming **is a worrying phenomenon**.
2) Beijing **is a very interesting city**.
3) **Nestled in the branches of the tree was** a raven.
4) **Tomorrow** we **are going to the cinema**.
5) **Waiting outside the shop was** the old man's dog.
6) The blood-red rose **was the glory of his garden**.

Answers to Quiz 82

1) Simple
2) Complex
3) Compound
4) Simple
5) Compound
6) Complex
7) Compound
8) Simple
9) Complex

Answers to Quiz 83

1) Non-restrictive clause
2) Restrictive clause
3) Restrictive clause
4) Non-restrictive clause
5) Restrictive clause
6) Non-restrictive clause

Answers to Quiz 84

1) Claire and Alison **are** two of the keenest dancers I know.
2) Our dog **is** a great entertainer.
3) Either Pete or Gordon **is** going to help you with your bags.
4) When I was growing up, both of my next-door neighbours **were** exceedingly kind.
5) Neither my mother nor my father **was** a very good swimmer.
6) I don't know anybody who **is** better at Scrabble than my Gran.
7) Everybody in the class **has** got a pass in the exam.
8) Several of my colleagues **have** tickets for the big concert.
9) Some cars **are** more fuel-efficient than others.
10) Some verse **is** difficult to read.
11) Fifty pounds **is** too much to pay for a dinner.
12) His rock band **is** being signed to a major label.
13) His team **are** going their separate ways at the end of the season.
14) Everyone in his school, as well as in all the other schools in the borough, **was** invited to perform at the arts festival.

Answers to Quiz 85

1) He hit **me** during our boxing bout.
2) You are much cleverer than **he**.
3) I like him far less than **her**.
4) I managed to make a cup of 'coffee' using gravy granules! Who else other than **I**?
5) That really is not for **me** to say.
6) I am a great fan of **them**.

Answers to Quiz 86

1) prepositional phrase
2) noun phrase
3) adverbial phrase
4) verb phrase
5) adjectival phrase
6) adverbial phrase
7) noun phrase
8) prepositional phrase
9) verb phrase
10) adjectival phrase
11) verb phrase
12) adverbial phrase
13) prepositional phrase
14) noun phrase
15) verb phrase
16) noun phrase
17) prepositional phrase
18) adjectival phrase
19) adverbial phrase
20) adjectival phrase

Answers to Quiz 87

1) b)
2) a)
3) a)
4) b)
5) b)
6) a)
7) a)
8) b)

Answers to Quiz 88

1) Is that chair free?
2) Was he late for his appointment?
3) Can't Bob go to the show?
4) Have you got a big house?
5) Has the post arrived?

Answers to Quiz 89

1) Does the bus go to the airport?
2) When does the bus leave?
3) What is the time?
4) Where does the bus leave from?
5) Which stop do you mean?
6) How much does a ticket cost?
7) How many passengers does the bus carry?
8) Who will check my ticket?
9) Are you going to the airport too?
10) Why are you going to the airport?

Answers to Quiz 90

1) **It's** the way of the world.
2) I have **fewer** hours free in the week now than I did when I was working full-time.
3) **There** was an old woman who lived in a shoe.
4) I don't understand **their** reasons for leaving.
5) I need to spend **less** money on taxis.
6) I don't know **who's** responsible for keeping the park tidy.
7) That is Steve, **whom** you met at the party at New Year.
8) The house, **which** was at the end of the street, suited him perfectly.
9) **They're** the most promising students in the whole year.
10) It was the lack of privacy **that** drove him to find a new place to live.
11) I could not see **its** point.
12) 'I like to know **whose** breakfast I'm eating,' said Goldilocks.

Answers to Quiz 91

1) My driving instructor told me to **practise** my night driving by picking up Little Johnny from his football practice.

2) 'Mobile phones are not **allowed** in class,' said the teacher **aloud** so that all the students could hear her.

3) When Fred noticed the hole in his **pail**, the colour drained from his face and he went quite **pale**.

4) The view from our **plane** was exquisite as we flew low over the **plain**.

5) Having **two** words that sound the same but that are spelled differently is just **too** confusing!

6) Our car was at this end of the car park but **their** car was over **there**.

7) She tried to walk **by** the shoe shop but when she saw those Manolo Blahnik's in the window, she knew she had to **buy** them.

8) 'We **accept** all forms of payment **except** credit cards,' said the shop's owner

9) My favourite watch has a strap that is too **loose** for me. I am afraid that I will **lose** it.

10) As our train stood **stationary** on the track, I penned a letter of complaint to the rail operator on my personalized **stationery**.

11) He knew the grammar quiz book might **affect** him emotionally but was surprised its **effect** lasted so long.

Answers to Quiz 92

1)	b)	across
2)	c)	accommodate
3)	b)	apparently
4)	c)	basically
5)	c)	business
6)	a)	committee
7)	b)	definitely
8)	b)	disappear
9)	a)	fluorescent
10)	a)	foreseeable
11)	b)	harassment
12)	b)	immediately
13)	c)	liaison
14)	a)	necessary
15)	c)	occurrence
16)	b)	preferred
17)	a)	remember
18)	a)	successful
19)	a)	tattoo
20)	c)	unfortunately

Answers to Quiz 93

1) She got the questions in the test **all right**.
2) He emerged from the crash unscathed and seemed completely **alright**.
3) Do you know if this chair is taken by **anyone**?
4) It could belong to **any one** of that crowd over there?
5) Having pooled our money, we had £80 **altogether**.
6) The United fans were in one pub while the City fans drank **all together** in another pub.
7) I **always** get lost in Rome.
8) **All ways** lead to Rome.
9) Her **everyday** life was lacking in excitement.
10) **Every day** I try to help someone.

11) He had catalogued **every one** of his CDs alphabetically.

12) **Everyone** has an opinion.

13) I was too scared to go **in to** see the reptiles.

14) The robbers broke **into** the bank.

15) **Maybe** someday I'll meet my one true love.

16) Though it **may be** that such a wonderful day will never arrive.

17) The man was tried for murder even though **no body** was ever found.

18) There was **nobody** there to answer the phone.

19) **Sometimes** I feel like starting a new life abroad.

20) The feeling hits me at **some times** more than others.

Answers to Quiz 94

1)	A.D. (anno domini)	e)	In the year of the Lord
2)	a.m. (ante meridiem)	j)	Before midday
3)	c.. (circa)	m)	Around / about / approximately
4)	cf. (confer)	s)	Bring together / compare
5)	CV (curriculum vitae)	k)	Course of life / account of one's life
6)	et al. (et alii)	o)	And others...
7)	etc. (et cetera)	n)	And the others / and other things
8)	e.g. (exempli gratia)	c)	For example
9)	ibid. (ibidem)	p)	In the same book / passage / article
10)	i.e. (id est)	r)	That is / in other words
11)	M.A. (magister artium)	t)	Master of arts
12)	M.O. (modus operandi)	i)	Method of operating
13)	N.B. (nota bene)	q)	Note well
14)	p.a. (per annum)	d)	For each year
15)	Ph.D. (philosophiæ doctor)	h)	Teacher of philosophy
16)	p.m. (post meridiem)	b)	After midday
17)	P.S. (post scriptum)	f)	After what has been written
18)	Q.E.D. (quod erat demonstrandum)	a)	Which was to be demonstrated
19)	R.I.P. (requiescat in pace)	g)	May he/she rest in peace
20)	viz. (videlicet)	l)	Namely / that is to say

Answers to Quiz 95

1) 10
2) 100
3) 500
4) 1
5) 50
6) 5
7) 1000

Answers to Quiz 96

Prefix		Meaning
1) a- / an- / in- / un- / non-	d)	not
2) ab-	j)	away, from
3) ad-	m)	changing into, moving towards, increasing
4) anti- / counter-	q)	opposing, against, the opposite
5) dis-	k)	indicating negation, removal, expulsion
6) extra-	r)	outside
7) hemi- / semi-	l)	half
8) hyper-	b)	more than, more than normal
9) inter-	e)	between, among
10) intra-	f)	inside, within
11) over-	g)	excessively, completely
12) post-	p)	after in time or order
13) pre- / ante-	n)	before, preceding
14) pro-	i)	favouring, in support of
15) re-	h)	again
16) sub-	a)	under, at a lower position
17) trans-	c)	across
18) ultra-	o)	beyond

Answers to Quiz 97

1) He did not believe in God. He was a self-proclaimed **atheist**.
2) Just as the opposition were attacking, Manchester United scored on the **counter-attack**.
3) The soldiers shot down the plane using their **anti-aircraft** gun.
4) Having spent much less on his campaign, the electoral candidate was at a serious **disadvantage**.
5) The little boy passed wind during the church service even though he knew it was **inappropriate**.
6) I wanted to stay sober so I had the **non-alcoholic** beer.
7) Having completed his journey he **dismounted** from his bicycle.
8) She considered his behaviour at the party, when he had made a pass at her mother, completely **unacceptable**.

Answers to Quiz 98

1) investigation
2) division
3) banker
4) victory
5) statistician
6) emptiness
7) placement
8) arrival

Answers to Quiz 99

1) lacy
2) sisterly
3) pitiful
4) incidental
5) reactionary
6) quotable

Answers to Quiz 100

1) Sydneysider
2) Neapolitan
3) Münchner
4) Muscovite
5) Capitalino
6) Liverpudlian
7) Vegan
8) Saigonese
9) Tapatío
10) Glaswegian
11) Florentine
12) Caraquenian
13) Capetonian
14) Cantabrigian
15) Bolognese

Answers to Quiz 101

1) variety of different
2) true fact
3) added bonus
4) climb up
5) complete opposite
6) very unique
7) honest truth
8) free gift
9) accidental mistake
10) end result

Answers to Quiz 102

1) a) achieve
2) a) aggressive
3) c) assassination
4) a) bizarre
5) b) colleague
6) a) conscious
7) c) dilemma
8) c) embarrass
9) c) foreign
10) a) government
11) a) humorous
12) b) independent
13) b) millennium
14) a) occasion
15) c) possession
16) b) receive
17) b) separate
18) c) supersede
19) a) tomorrow
20) b) wherever

Answers to Quiz 103

1) Between you and **me**, this sentence seems perfectly fine to me. (Following the preposition, the personal pronoun acts as the object and thus should be in the accusative case.)

2) If I **were** you, I would do all I could to take full marks in the exam. (Here we have a second conditional, which cries out for the subjunctive.)

3) An average of 50,000 people **attends** games at the new stadium. (When referring to 'an average of...', you should use the singular form of the verb).

4) **Fewer** than fifteen people have stepped on the moon.
(When referring to a countable noun without a specific number, opt for *fewer* rather than *less*.)

5) **Owing to** the absence of rain, all the plants in my garden perished.
(A very subtle stylistic point that most of the modern world ignores. To choose which phrase to use, bear in mind the following rule: *owing to* in effect replaces the phrase *because of* while *due to* stands in for *caused by*.)

6) Nancy Mitford was the **oldest** of the six Mitford sisters.
(As there are 'more than two' in the group of sisters, you need to use the superlative here.)

7) The defendant's explanation for his presence at the crime scene did not bear **scrutiny**.
(*Close scrutiny* is a classic example of a tautological phrase.)

8) **It's** none of my concern **who's** been given the job instead of me.
(Two 'incorrect forms' – *it* and *who* should not be in the possessive case here. Instead *it's* and *who's* are contractions of *it is* and *who has*.)

9) I question if there is enough grammar education in schools.
(Though a question is being posed, it is indirect and does not require a question mark at the end of the sentence.)

10) Running across the beach, **Pamela cut her foot on** a large, jagged shell.
(It was not the shell that was running across the beach, though that is what is suggested by the misplaced participle in the original.)

11) I think, therefore I am.
    (Without the comma after *think*, 'therefore I am' appears to be
    just a rather random thought that I had.)

12) The patient had an infection and needed antibiotics, so the
    doctor **prescribed** some for her.
    (A simple case of wrong word selection. *To proscribe* means
    to forbid.)

13) He looked very fine in his new dress-shirt and jacket.
    (A crucial hyphen helps us to understand that *he* was wearing
    a traditional item of male apparel and removes any doubt as to
    whether *he* was sporting a frock of some sort.)

14) It was not my intention to end the book on a low note, so
    I hope this is not too enraging a quiz **with which** to have
    left you.
    (Wherever possible, aim to avoid ending a sentence – or indeed
    a book – with a preposition. However, just occasionally you
    can get away with it if the alternative sounds silly. As Winston
    Churchill is said to have once quipped: 'Ending a sentence with
    a preposition is something up with which I will not put.')